A CIVIL WAR CAMPAIGN THROUGH MISSOURI

Recollections of a German Soldier

Including the
Original German Transcript

A CIVIL WAR CAMPAIGN THROUGH MISSOURI

Recollections of a German Soldier

Including the
Original German Transcript

Compiled by Dennis Hood

Translated and Introduced by Stephen Trobisch

Edited by Cynthia Johnson

Leonard Press
Bolivar, MO

Bolivar, Missouri Copyright ©2012 by Dennis Hood. All rights reserved. Printed in the United States of America. No part of this book may be used or reproduced in any manner whatsoever without written permission except in the case of brief quotations embodied in critical articles and reviews.

Leonard Press
Bolivar, MO 65613-0752

For other titles, prices, and order information:
www.leonardpress.com
info@leonardpress.com

ISBN 978-1-931475-59-4
Library of Congress Control Number: 2012940615

Cover Design by Cynthia Johnson
Map: "Map of the Seat of War in the West," *Harper's Weekly*, September 7, 1861.
Poster: Missouri State Guard recruiting poster, from the collection of Dennis Hood.
Photograph: August Reimers, Officer of the Fifteenth Missouri Volunteer Regiment, from the collection of Dennis Hood.

Table of Contents

Introduction i
Charles J. Kopp's Song 1
Recollections 5

Missouri
Rolla, February 1, 1862 11
Big Piney River, February 3, 1862 18
Waynesville, February 4, 1862 21
Lebanon, February 6, 1862 27
Lebanon, Continued 31
Marshfield, February 11, 1862 36
Springfield, February 13, 1862 41
Wilson's Creek, February 14, 1862 52
Little York, February 14, 1862 54
Cassville, Ceatsville, February 16, 1862 61

Arkansas
Pea Ridge, February 19, 1862 64
Sugar Creek, Bentonville, February 19, 1862 66

Commentary of the Transcriber 77
Poem in Honor of Siblings 79
Original German Transcript 81
Index 136

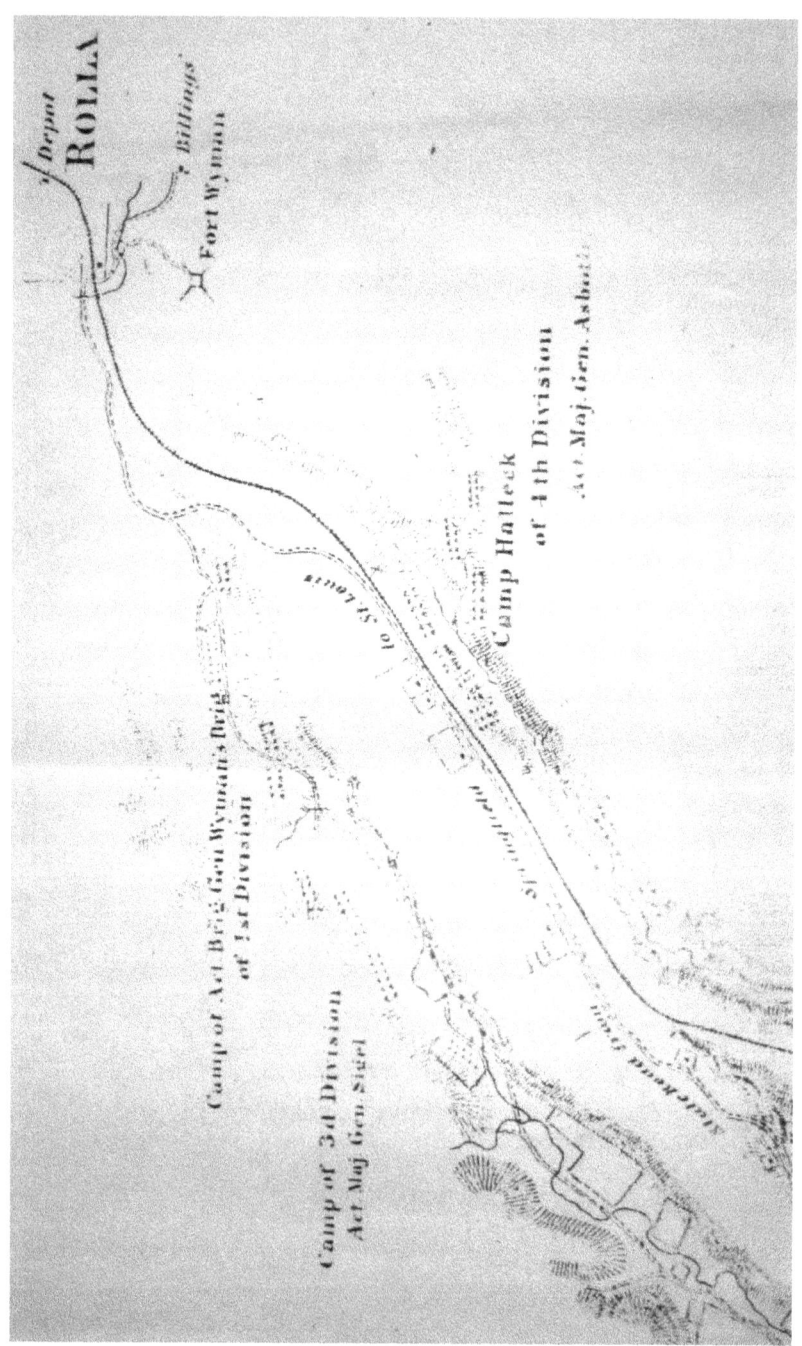

Figure 1. Map of winter quarters in Rolla before the campaign, Dec. 1861. Map courtesy of Dennis Hood.

TABLE OF FIGURES

Figure 1. Map of Winter Quarters in Rolla
Figure 2. Original German Manuscript v
Figure 3. Missouri State Guard Recruiting Poster x
Figure 4. Major Charles Zagonyi xi
Figure 5. "Old Friend" Photograph xiv
Figure 6. Charles Kopp's Song, Page 1 1
Figure 7. Charles Kopp's Song, Page 2 2
Figure 8. General Samuel R. Curtis 7
Figure 9. *Liberty Tribune* 8
Figure 10. Original German Manuscript 10
Figure 11. General Fremont and General Sigel 19
Figure 12. Lebanon, Missouri 33
Figure 13. General Franz Sigel 35
Figure 14. *Rolla Express* 37
Figure 15. *Liberty Tribune* 40
Figure 16. Springfield, Missouri 42
Figure 17. Original German Manuscript 44
Figure 18. General Jim Lane 45
Figure 19. General Sterling Price 50
Figure 20. Map of Little York 55
Figure 21. Hard Tack 57
Figure 22. Battle of Pea Ridge 65
Figure 23. General Ben McCulloch 67
Figure 24. A Texas Ranger 68

Acknowledgements

For their valuable contributions, distinguished expertise, and continuous support, we wish to express our heartfelt thanks to:

John Bradbury

Mark Douglas Dillow

Oliver Günther

Dennis Hood

Cynthia Johnson

Jeff Patrick

Klaus Trobisch

INTRODUCTION
BY STEPHEN TROBISCH

This book contains the recollections of a Civil War campaign through Missouri by a German soldier in early 1862. It serves as a reminder that European immigrants participated in significant numbers in the American Civil War. Over 20 percent of all Union soldiers were German-American, and more than one-third of them were born in Germany. Many of these "Dutchmen"—as they were often called—had been schooled and educated in Germany. Not only did they write their letters, journals, and reminiscences in German, they also communicated in their native language during their arduous campaigns and military engagements. The American Civil War was therefore also *European,* and it was fought by individuals still trying to discover America and find their own identities within their new country.

I believe that the perspectives and firsthand experiences of *Europeans* may still be understudied in the histories of the American Civil War. I have also found that narratives of Civil War battles and campaigns west of the Mississippi are less prominently represented in general studies—such as in the 1990 PBS television series, *The Civil War,* by Ken Burns—compared to the narratives of the renowned battles at locations to the east, such as Vicksburg, Gettysburg, Richmond, and Atlanta, and those of the legendary protagonists, such as Jackson, Lee, Sherman, and Grant. Earl Hess has pointed out that the battles of Wilson's Creek, Pea Ridge, and Prairie Grove were three of the most significant engagements of the Civil War west of the Mississippi, as they helped shape Union military efforts to control the Trans-Mississippi and "were absolutely vital in maintaining the relentless Union pressure in the western theater."

This book attempts to present a succinctly German perspective on a military campaign through Missouri in early 1862 (in the wake of Missouri's momentous Battle of Wilson's Creek in August, 1861), even before much of the Civil War drama began to unfold in the eastern theaters. While Germans formed most of General Lyon's army and were prominent under General Fremont at Wilson's Creek, they represented only one division out of three at Pea Ridge. Their influence in Missouri affairs, therefore, was limited. Some evidence suggests that by 1864, German citizens were being singled out for retribution by guerrillas and bushwhackers in central Missouri. This, however, may be the subject for another treatise. Since these wartime accounts and reminiscences were written in German, many of them might still be waiting to be discovered and translated.

Among the *Europeans* in the Union Army of the Southwest were German immigrants as well as first and second generation Germans from Iowa, Ohio, Indiana, and Illinois, the homestate of Abraham Lincoln. Many Germans felt naturally motivated to fight for the cause of the Union, as they revered President Lincoln and regarded themselves agents for the cause of preventing secession of Confederate States, including the bordering state of Missouri. A good number of these Germans came from families who had left Germany in the wake of the unsuccessful revolution of 1848. Now, however, they found themselves in another conflict, often gauging similar values that motivated their migration to America in the first place. While the author of the *Recollections* does represent a decidedly *Northern* point of view, he is also critical of the Union army's operational practices, and he does not endow his narrative with a particular sense of nationalism or religion.

Challenges of the Original Manuscript

Over a decade ago, Dennis Hood presented me with an antiquated binder containing German manuscripts about a Civil War campaign through Missouri. I perused the material with tremendous interest. I had been working on letter-collections written by German soldiers during World Wars I and II, and I was surprised how the literary voices of these German soldiers struck similar chords and followed analogous sentiments in spite of the vastly removed scenarios in place and time. From between the lines emerges a passion for describing not only the events of the campaign, but also the personal interpretations and insights endowed with philosophical and even poetic facets. The author of the *Recollections* displays skill and versatility in his writing, and most importantly, a compelling need for verbal expression of a momentous experience in his life. All these aspects I regard as substantive ingredients of meaningful literature.

Reading the material, however, I immediately recognized a multitude of challenges: deciphering and transcribing the handwriting, translating the text from German into English, searching for the identity of the author who stubbornly refuses to make revealing references about himself, validating the events from other sources, bringing two parallel narratives into a coherent presentation, determining the genre, etc.

In the following I will briefly discuss these aspects and the progression of bringing the manuscript to publication, preliminary as it may be. I also want to suggest from the outset that—since this book is not yet "finished"—we already anticipate a second edition that will contain more informed responses to questions which, for now, had to remain unanswered. Hopefully, some resourceful contributions by our readers will offer further revelations.

Transcription

One entire draft of the manuscript had been penned in *Deutscher Kurrentschrift,* a German "script" that was the nineteenth-century standard of cursive handwriting using fountain pens with a pointed steel nib. While the reading through larger sections of the manuscript posed few challenges, the deciphering of some words and idiomatic expressions took considerable effort. The reason lay not only in the individual peculiarity and legibility of the handwriting itself and in the author's inconsistent orthography, but in the encroaching verbiage of the English-speaking environment that increasingly affected the author after having left Germany presumably at a younger age, probably soon after completing his secondary education. While entire regiments of the Southwest army communicated largely in German during their campaigns, words like "Framehouse," "Fence," or "Husher" (a reference to *hoosiers* in an anglicized German spelling; nevertheless, capitalized as all German nouns) had become standard vernacular. With the privilege of the assistance of my uncle, Klaus Trobisch—who had practiced *Kurrentschrift* when schooled in the 1940s in Germany—we were able to decipher and transcribe each of these linguistic challenges. For readers interested in nineteenth-century German usage—particularly that of the American Civil War—this book presents an original documentation. The transcription of the German narrative is printed in its entirety in the final section of this book.

    I have then drafted an English translation with some emphasis on retaining literal and syntactical German attributes. Cynthia Johnson, our editor, worked in painstaking detail on producing a readable English prose while cautiously retaining a touch of the German character in its narrative presentation. She also searched for precise formulations and appropriate English equivalencies of nineteenth-century German colloquialisms and their archaic figures of speech. For further clarification, I have added footnotes for several of these translations. German readers will be able to read the original in the final section of the book or to reference it as needed. While the endeavor of translation will never truly be "finished," we proudly present this text to our American readers. We also encourage critical responses, and we would be pleased to acknowledge and incorporate them in the second edition of this book.

Parallel Narratives
The account is presented in two drafts: one is composed in *Deutscher Kurrentschrift*; the other in cursive Latin script, written probably at a later time. While the second draft contains large portions of the first draft, it has several new details and paragraphs added while other elements of the first draft are left out.

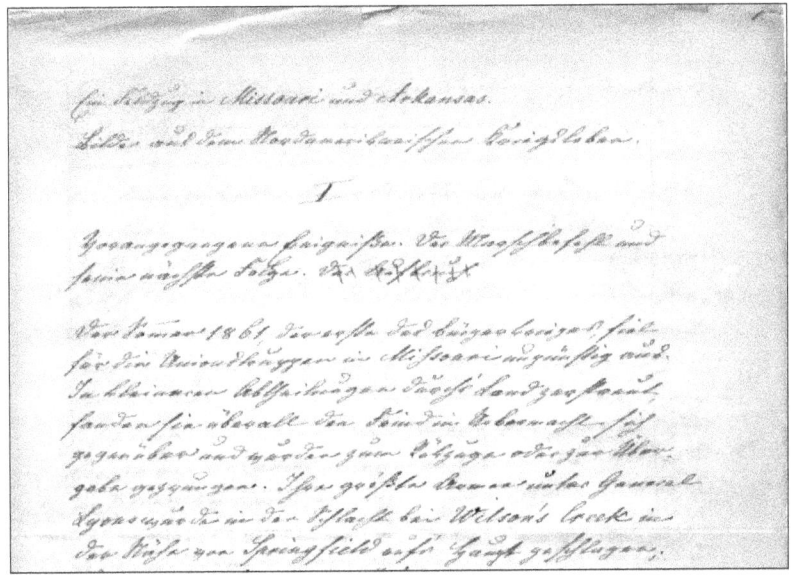

Figure 2. Image of the original manuscript in German Kurrentschrift.

Both narratives are parallel. They describe the military campaign starting in Rolla, Missouri, on February 2, 1862, and its progression through Waynesville, Lebanon, and Marshfield to Springfield, Missouri, roughly along the route that would become Highway 66 and eventually Interstate 44. And while the second draft ends with the arrival in Springfield on February 14, 1862, the first draft goes on to describe the continued pursuit of the "Rebel army" to Arkansas. It ends with a description of a family farm in Arkansas and of the town of Keetsville (or Keatsville, near present-day Cassville) where large numbers of both armies' wounded had been accommodated after the Battle of Pea Ridge. Both narratives end with paragraphs that suggest the author's intent to bring each of the respective accounts to a conclusion. The reader, however, is left with open questions about the author's reason for ending the narrative at such points in time and about his possible engagements in other campaigns throughout the Civil War. It is conceivable that the manuscripts at hand may have been only a portion of a larger whole which the author had planned but not completed. It is also conceivable that more sections have been written but not yet found. Perhaps new insights by our readers will shed some light on these speculations.

We first considered publishing both drafts separately and in sequence. Cynthia Johnson, however, suggested that the narratives might be superimposed to avoid redundancies. She then put together a version that is inclusive of all details of both texts—bracketing the insertions of the "other narrative"—while preserving the linear and chronological progression of the account free of cumbersome repetitions.

Authorship

Another nearly intractable challenge and source of some frustration is our continued search for the identity of the author. While he offers reliable references about the generals of the Army of the Southwest (Curtis, Osterhaus, Asboth, Sigel, Davis, and Carr) during the campaign from February to March of 1862, he staunchly resists revelations about himself or about the names of his immediate companions, superiors, or subordinates.

Mark Douglas Dillow has offered his invaluable assistance to us, together with his expert insight in matters of American military. Examining the material, Dillow observed that the author appears to have had light duty and available time to write, along with requisite education. Therefore, he may have not been a Unit Commander, but perhaps a Staff Officer, an Adjutant, a Surgeon, or a Quartermaster. Discussing trading for food and reimbursements to civilians for requisitioned supplies may suggest that he was a Quartermaster. The description of the dialogue with the secessionist doctor, who was left behind with the wounded in Springfield, may suggest that he had medical inclinations. After careful analysis of listings of the Fifteenth Infantry, Missouri Volunteers, Dillow suggests that three candidates emerge as somewhat likely to be the author: Quartermaster Charles Peret, Adjutant George Hollman, and Surgeon William Steiger. We were, however, not able to associate reliably any of these names with the identity of the author. Compounding the mystery is the fact that, as Dillow pointed out to us, only officers (Majors, Lt. Col., Col.) would have horses in infantry units. And, indeed, the author frequently makes reference about riding his horse, taking care of it, and even writing his *journal* while sitting in the saddle and waiting for the convoy to get moving.

To make the search even more enigmatic, a tantalizing document was attached to the binder containing the German originals, namely, a poem written to honor one *Alexander*. The poem was performed for the occasion of Alexander visiting his family in Germany after the Civil War. The poem is signed by the initials "F. R." and the poem's author may have been one of Alexander's siblings. Whether Alexander, to whom this poem is dedicated, is also the author of the *Recollections*, we could not verify. Whether the initial "R," refers to Alexander's last name is purely speculative, since the poem may have been authored by a married sister or by a member of the extended family. We have added the poem at the end of the *Recollections*. Again, we invite interested readers to assist us in the search. For now, we took the liberty to endow our anonymous author arbitrarily with the name *Alexander* even though the records of the

Fifteenth Infantry, Missouri Volunteers, award an uncertain likelihood of this being the author's actual name.

A Journal?

Even though Alexander entitles the second narrative—that ending with the arrival in Springfield—with "Journal of a Missouri-Volunteer," only some characteristics of a journal—in the sense of a daily record kept within sequential chronology—are observed. While Alexander does indicate dates for certain sections, he often flashes forward and also backward employing grander historical perspectives. Some of these could have only been known after the outcome of future events. In an entry of February 19, 1862, for instance, Alexander refers to the aftermath of the Battle of Pea Ridge which took place at the beginning of March, 1862.

Alexander probably did use a journal when writing down the account originally, but he abandoned its arrangement when rewriting the two drafts, probably after the Civil War ended. Therefore, we opted to label the manuscript *Recollections* and to insert sub-headers to orient the reader in terms of the exact place and time of the military campaign. These sub-headers make the narrative easy to follow.

Sources Corroborating Alexander's Account

In our search for Alexander's identity, we found two sources which corroborate several of the descriptions of the *Recollections*. These are the accounts by William Burns[1] and by August

---

[1] He had been promised a position by Alexander S. Asboth in 1861 and received a lieutenant's commission in the "Fremont Hussars," which later became the 4th Missouri Cavalry. Burns was acquainted with Capt. B. C. Ludlow and moved to Rolla on December 30, joining his Company C with Captain Eugene von Kielmansegge.

Reimers.[2] Details of their stories confirm those of Alexander who may have even been acquainted with one or both of them. The following briefly lists striking parallels of Burns' and Reimers' accounts to that of Alexander.

William Burns
 Mud in the Tent
  "Here we are among the Ozark mountains, sixty miles from Rolla. I am seated on my camp cot, in a crowded tent, my paper on my knee, and my feet on empty oat sacks to keep them out of the mud; otherwise I am quite comfortable." [Burns, William S. *Recollections of the 4th Missouri Cavalry.* Dayton, OH: Morningside House, 1988. p. 17]

 Order to March to Bolivar
  "Order came to march to Bolivar to aid a camp in fear of an attack. Febr. 6th, bivouacked within fifteen miles of Bolivar, entered the town, but found no rebels." [p. 20]

---

[2] He was born in Schwerin, Mecklenburg, Germany in 1841. After his father's death, his mother migrated with her children to America. She died in St. Louis in 1852, when August was only eleven years old. He became a candy maker's apprentice in St. Louis. He entered military service as a private, Company B, Fifteenth Missouri Volunteer Infantry and Third Missouri Volunteer Infantry, for three months and fought at the Battle of Wilson's Creek where he was injured. After recovery he mustered out and reenlisted as a private, Company E of the Fifteenth Missouri Volunteer Infantry. He moved to Rolla until February 1862 and then advanced on Springfield, February 2–13, and in pursuit of General Price, he marched to Bentonville, Arkansas, and fought at the Battle of Pea Ridge, March 7–8. August Reimers was in Asboth's Brigade and in Sigel's Division.

WAR, WAR! WAR!!

The following telegraphic DISPATCH Has just been RECEIVED:

JEFFERSON CITY, MO., May, 16, 1861

"COL. J. F. SNYDER,
                Bolivar, Mo :
Send us a good Company well armed.
          STERLING PRICE, Commander-in-Chief.

All who wish to enlist are requested to meet in **BOLIVAR** on Saturday next, 18th. Each recruit is expected to bring a blanket and a good rifle, and be prepared to leave on Sunday morning. As soon as the Company is formed, officers will be elected and the Company will march at once.
Bolivar, Mo., 16th.

Figure 3. Missouri State Guard Recruiting Poster.
Bolivar, Missouri, May 1861. Photo courtesy of Dennis Hood.

March on Springfield, February 11–12

"Just as we arrived at camp that evening, within twelve miles of Springfield, we heard the sound of cannon ahead, and in a few moments a messenger came rushing into our camp, with orders from Gen. Sigel for us to hurry forward, as he, with the advance guard, had been attacked. We were soon in our saddles again, and with Gen. Asboth and staff, were hurrying to the front.... It seems that Gen. Sigel had run into 500 or 600 of Price's men, who opened fire upon him, to which he replied from a couple of howitzers, and scattered them.... To be sure, our return was quiet and orderly, but we passed artillery, cavalry and infantry turning round and generally mixed together." [p. 20]

"When within five miles of Springfield... we heard, to our surprise, that [Price] had retreated, and the party to whom Gen. Sigel had paid the shelling salutation the previous evening, was Price's rearguard, covering his retreat." (February 12) [p. 21]

Arrival in Springfield

"About noon we marched through Springfield, passed the spot where Major Zagonyi made his bold charge at the head of the 'Freemont Body Guard,' and pitched our tents where stood the barracks so hastily deserted the night before by the Missouri traitors." [p. 21]

Little York

"Nine miles from Springfield, we passed through the village of Little York, and I there saw, lying by the roadside, my first dead rebel (if he was a rebel). He had been killed the night

Figure 4. Major Zagonyi.
Photo courtesy of Dennis Hood.

xi

before, by our company 'A,' which had been sent out scouting, and came upon what I have always had good reason to believe was a party of refugees. Our men supposing them to be the rear of Price's army, attacked them, killing eight and capturing about twenty wagons, and there was this poor fellow lying by the roadside where he fell." [p. 23]

Camp near Wilson's Creek and Keatsville
"We encamped that night six miles west of the historic 'Wilson's Creek.' During the next day's march we caught sight of baggage wagons moving far in advance. One company started in pursuit, and brought back eleven wagons, and one carriage in which was a wounded rebel captain.... The next day Generals Curtis and Sigel joined forces again, and encamped that night at Cassville, but we, being with Gen. Asboth, being the advance guard, encamped seven miles ahead of them at Keatsville. We waited next morning for the arrival of the two generals, and then the whole army, about twelve thousand strong, advanced together." [p. 23]

Elk Horn Tavern
"During our march this day, we passed a roadside tavern, upon the roof of which was fastened a magnificent pair of deer horns, which gave it the name of 'Elk Horn Tavern.' The battle fought by us, about two weeks later, known as 'Pea Ridge,' was called by the Southerners, the 'Battle of Elk Horn.'" [p. 23]

Sugar Creek
"...we encamped at 'Sugar Creek,' and learned the cause of all the late noise and excitement. Our troops had come upon the rear guard of Price's army strongly posted on a bluff, with four pieces of artillery. The result was an artillery duel, forcing the enemy to continue their retreat, leaving, however, nine of our men dead on the field, and fifteen of the rebels captives in our hands." [p. 24]

Bentonville

"The next day, the main army remained in camp, but 250 of us rode over to Bentonville, a village ten miles to the west. We entered Bentonville on the full gallop and captured several prisoners, and some confederate stores, and the Fourth Missouri Cavalry had the credit of capturing the first secession flag taken in Arkansas.... and we reached camp soon after dark. We all remained in camp at 'Sugar Creek' next day resting (February 19)." [p. 24]

Poisoning of Louis Dulfer

"The morning after our arrival, Capt.... [Louis Dulfer], of our regiment, was poisoned, and in half an hour was dead. Several others were also poisoned, but after much suffering recovered. An account of this affair was sent east by a newspaper correspondent as an attempt by the Southerners to poison our whole army; that they had poisoned their wells, etc., etc. The facts were, Capt [Dulfer] and others broke open a deserted drugstore, and drank some poison, instead of liquor which they were after. We buried our dead captain by starlight in a beautiful spot, in 'Cross Hollow,' but in a wild and lonely grave, Gen. Asboth acting as the chaplain."
[p. 24f]

Battle of Pea Ridge

"But at this moment up came that brave old Hungarian, Gen. Asboth with the 2d Ohio battery (in which was Lieut. Conrad Gansevoort, of our own village of Bath) and a few companies of infantry, and changed the heart of affairs, and saved the day.

"Gen. Sigel was on the move all night (7th-8th) arranging his men for the morrow's work. Our Major was sick (but his was with the 'white feather')[3] ... but we found a good commander in my old Captain Kielmansegge, who was then on General Sigel's staff." [p. 34f]

---

[3] A mark of cowardice.

Keetsville

"Next morning (9th) we advanced to Keetsville, where we learned that the rebels had left the main road and dispersed in all directions, so we returned to our old camp at Sugar Creek that evening. It was hard to believe that we had been victorious (gaining one of the greatest victories of the war, at that date), as they had us completely surrounded…" [p. 35]

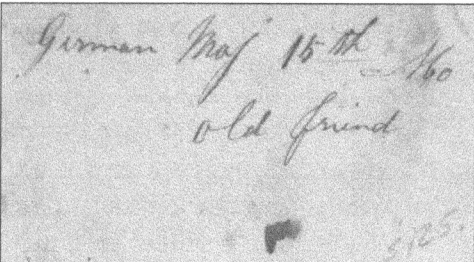

Figure 5. "Old Friend." A photograph of a German major in the Fifteenth Missouri Volunteer Regiment, the back of which reads, "German Maj 15th Mo / old friend." Photo courtesy of Dennis Hood.

August Reimers[4]

Snowstorm at the Outset of the Campaign from Rolla

"In February we marched away to the Southwest on the campaign which terminated in the Battle of Pea Ridge. It was fearful weather, and the first night out it snowed about six inches. When we got into camp, the roads were rough, and our teams could not come up, so we camped in a cornfield,[5]

---

[4] At first we speculated whether August Reimers might have authored the *Recollections*. Upon learning that he had migrated to the United States at the age of nine or ten, it became clear that he could not have received the German schooling necessary to employ the eloquent literary references present in Alexander's narrative.

[5] That same night, Alexander had the privilege to spend the night in one of the log-houses located on that farm.

with nothing but our haversacks to fall back upon, and snowing for all it was worth." [Rekkas, Sue. "August Reimers." *IAGenWeb Project*.]

"Three of us in my company... gathered up a lot of corn stalks, spread a blanket on the stakes, lay down and covered ourselves with the other two blankets and slept all night."

"During the night our wagons had come up, and we made some hot coffee in the morning. About 10 o'clock we started on our march again."

Elkhorn Tavern
"There was considerable skirmishing on the 6th and on the 7th some heavy fighting. My Regiment was kept in reserve most of the time. On the 8th, Franz Sigel concentrated his artillery on the Elkhorn Tavern road and got to Confederates in a cross fire. When we charged, they broke and ran, and we after them."

Generals Fremont and Wallenstein

While camped in Springfield after the Battle of Wilson's Creek, Alexander draws several analogies between General Fremont and the legendary German general of the seventeenth-century Thirty Years' War: Wallenstein. In his classic German tragedy, Friedrich Schiller treats the downfall of this well-known General Wallenstein. At the peak of his fame and power, Wallenstein begins to dissent against his commander, the Emperor Ferdinand II. Eventually Wallenstein is sentenced to death.

The first part of the trilogy—"Wallenstein's Camp"—begins during the winter of 1633/34 (nearly sixteen years into the Thirty Years' War) in the Bohemian town of Pilsen where Wallenstein camps with his troops. This is the scenario from which Alexander derives the analogies to Fremont's camp in Springfield, Missouri, in the wake of the Battle of Wilson's Creek. Schiller's drama reflects the mood among the nonaristocratic sentiments of the soldiers in the camp. They love their commander who managed to create a formidable fighting force with soldiers originating from many sections of the empire that were divided by language and culture. The soldiers are in praise of Wallenstein who had granted them liberties not previously enjoyed under the direct rule of the Emperor. The soldiers in Schiller's drama also celebrate war which promises a better future. A monk, however, emerges in the camp, criticizing the godless life of the soldiers in one of the classic soliloquies in German literature.[6]

Und die Armee liegt hier in Böhmen, Pflegt den Bauch, läßt sich's wenig grämen, Kümmert sich mehr um den Krug als den Krieg, Wetzt lieber den Schnabel als den Sabel ...	And the army lies here in Bohemia, tends to the stomach without being troubled, worried more about the pitcher than the war, rather sharpens the tongue than the sword…

Alexander is quite unabashed in his praise of General Fremont. When describing his quarters in Springfield, Missouri, he elevates Fremont's prominence to that of the fabled General Wallenstein. History, however, has shed a less flattering light on General Fremont. After he imposed martial law in the state of Missouri in August 1861, he confiscated secessionists' private property and evoked the emancipation of slaves. For fear of driving Missouri and other slave states in Union control to the Southern cause, President Lincoln asked Fremont to revise the order. After Fremont's refusal, Lincoln revoked the proclamation and relieved Fremont of command in November 1861.

---

[6] Alexander uses a part of the monk's soliloquy to describe unfortunate circumstances in the winter camp in Rolla.

In spite of his admiration for Fremont and the allusions to Wallenstein, Alexander stops short of comparing President Lincoln to Emperor Ferdinand II. Nevertheless, Alexander re-invokes the monk's sentiments when describing the idle camp in Rolla during the winter of 1861/62 after the Union army had relinquished already-occupied Missouri territory between Springfield and Rolla to the Confederates, and he thus expresses displeasure at the Union upper command.

Die Süd-West Armee aber lag 2½ Monat lang, von Mitte November bis Ende Januar, theils in Baracken, theils unter Zelten, bey Rolla auf dem Schnee und auf der faulen Haut—	The Army of the Southwest, however, lay for 2½ months, from mid-November until the end of January, partly in barracks and partly under tents, idly on the snow in Rolla—
▪ *kümmerte sich mehr um den Krug als den Krieg,*	▪ concerned more about the bottle than the war,
▪ *wetzte lieber den Schnabel als den Sabel,*	▪ sharpening the tongue rather than the saber,
▪ *dachte nur an Trank und Speis,*	▪ and only thinking of drink and food,
▪ *und gab Price Missouri preis.*	▪ while exposing the Missouri prize to General Price.

Alexander clearly added the last two lines to the Schiller soliloquy, giving voice not only to a sense of frustration about the Union army's retreat to Rolla in November 1861, but also indicating a remarkable ability to improvise lines in variation to German classic literature.

Charles Kopp's Ode to His Coat

Charles Kopp represents another example of a German immigrant with a remarkable ability for lyrical literary expression who found himself fighting in the American Civil War. Perusing the collections of Dennis Hood, we found this remarkable *Song* and thought that it would illustrate the extraordinary artistry in writing among German Civil War soldiers, although Charles Kopp is otherwise not associated with Alexander. The *Ode to His Coat* describes a most trusted and comforting item of clothing that continues to instill security and shelter—a sense of home, perhaps—in the hostile and dangerous circumstance of war and new country. The reader may forgive the imperfect English translation which attempted to capture the *Song's* literal meaning line by line of the otherwise far more lyrical German original. Following Charles Kopp's *Ode* are Alexander's *Recollections*.

We hope that this book will provide not only an enlightening contribution to German chronicles of the American Civil War, but also an opportunity to read about the various Civil War localities in Missouri and Arkansas for readers with regional interests. To the readers of *A Civil War Campaign through Missouri*, we extend the invitation to shed more light on the speculations mentioned above. We would be honored to hear from you.

Dr. Stephen Trobisch

Selected Bibliography

Allendorf, Donald. *Long Road to Liberty: The Odyssey of a German Regiment in the Yankee Army—the 15th Missouri Volunteer Infantry.* Kent, OH: Kent State University Press, 2006.

Angus, Fern. *Down the Wire Road in the Missouri Ozarks.* Marionville, MO: Fern Angus, 1992.

Banasik, Michael E. (Ed.) *Missouri Brothers in Gray: Unwritten Chapters of the Civil War West of the River.* Volume I. Iowa City, IA: Camp Pope Bookshop, 1998.

Banasik, Michael E. (Author / Ed.) *Reluctant Cannoneer: The Diary of Robert T. McMahan of the Twenty-fifth Independent Ohio Light Artillery.* Iowa City, IA: Camp Pope Bookshop, 2000.

Bartels, Carolyn. *Pea Ridge: the Sacrifice.* Independence, MO: Two Trails Publishing, (privately published).

Britton, Wiley. *Memoirs of the Rebellion on the Border, 1863.* Lincoln, NE: University of Nebraska Press: 1993.

Brophy, Patrick (Ed.) *"Found No Bushwhackers": The 1864 Diary of Sgt. James P. Mallery.* Nevada, MO: Vernon County Historical Society, 1988.

Brophy, Patrick (Ed.) *In the Devil's Dominions: A Union Soldier's Adventures in "Bushwhacker Country". The Journal of Charles W. Porter, Lieutenant, afterwards Captain, Co. F, 3rd Wisconsin Cavalry, Stationed in Southwest Missouri 1862-1865.* Nevada, MO: Vernon County Historical Society, 1998.

Burns, William S. *Recollections of the 4th Missouri Cavalry.* Dayton, OH: Morningside House, 1988.

Davis, Kathleen (Ed.) *Such Are the Trails: The Civil War Diaries of Jacob Gantz.* Ames, IA: Iowa State University Press, 1991.

Dennis, Frank Allen (Ed.). *Recollections of the 4th Missouri Cavalry by William Burns, Captain Co. 1, 4th Missouri Cavalry (Union).* Dayton, OH: Morningside, 1988.

Engle, Stephen D. *Yankee Dutchman: The Life of Franz Sigel.* Fayetteville: University of Arkansas Press, 1993.

Fitzhugh, Lester N. (Ed.) *Cannon Smoke: the Letters of Captain John J. Good, Good-Douglas Texas Battery, CSA.* Hillsboro, TX: The Hill Junior College Press, 1971.

Gammage, W. L. (Brigade Surgeon). *The Camp, the Bivouac, and the Battle Field: A History of the Fourth Arkansas Regiment, from its First Organization Down to the Present Date. Its Campaigns and its Battles with an Occasional Reference to the Current Events of the Times, Including Biographical Sketches of its Field Officers and Others of the Old Brigade.* Selma, AR: Arkansas Southern Press, 1958.

Hale, Douglas. *The Third Texas Cavalry in the Civil War.* Norman, OK: University of Oklahoma Press, 1993.

Hatcher, Richard W. and William Garrett Piston (Eds.) *Kansans at Wilson's Creek: Soldier's Letters from the Campaign for Southwest Missouri.* Springfield, MO: Wilson's Creek National Battlefield Foundation, 1993.

Hess, Earl J., et. al. *Wilson's Creek, Pea Ridge, and Prarie Grove: A Battlefield Guide with a Section on the Wire Road.* Lincoln, NE: University of Nebraska Press, 2006.

Huff, Leo E. (Ed.) *The Civil War Letters of Albert Demuth and Roster Eighth Missouri Volunteer Cavalry.* Springfield, MO: Green County Historical Society, 1997.

Kautz, August V. (Capt. Sixth U.S. Cavalry, Brig.-Gen. U.S. Volunteers). *Customs of Service for Non-Commissioned Officers and Soldiers as Derided from Law and Regulations and Practised in the Army of the United States.* Philadelphia, N.J: J. B. Lippincott & Co., 1864.

Lenox, David F. *Personal Memoirs of a Missouri Confederate Soldier and His Commentaries on the Race and Liquor Question.* Texarkana, TX: 1905.

Patrick, Jeff (Ed.) *Nine Months in the Infantry Service: The Civil War Journal of R. P. Matthews and Roster, The Phelps Regiment Missouri Volunteers.* Springfield, MO: Greene County Historical Society, 1999.

Phillips, J. K. (Ed.) *Memoirs of an Ozark Pioneer and Civil War Soldier: Private James Frances Coatney, First Arkansas Union Cavalry, Company D.* Berryville, AR: Jakie Spring, 2008.

Rekkas, Sue. "August Reimers." *IAGenWeb Project.*

Rowan, Steven (Transl. / Ed.) *Germans for a Free Missouri: Translations from the St. Louis Radical Press, 1857-1862.* Columbia, MO: University of Missouri Press, 1983.

Schiller, Friedrich. *Wallenstein.* Frankfurt: Insel, 1984.

Tunnard, W. H. and Edwin C. Bearss. *A Southern Record: The History of the Third Regiment Louisiana Infantry.* Dayton, OH: Morningside, 1988.

Watson, William. *Life in the Confederate Army: Observations and Experiences of an Alien in the South During the American Civil War.* New York: Scribner and Welford, 1888.

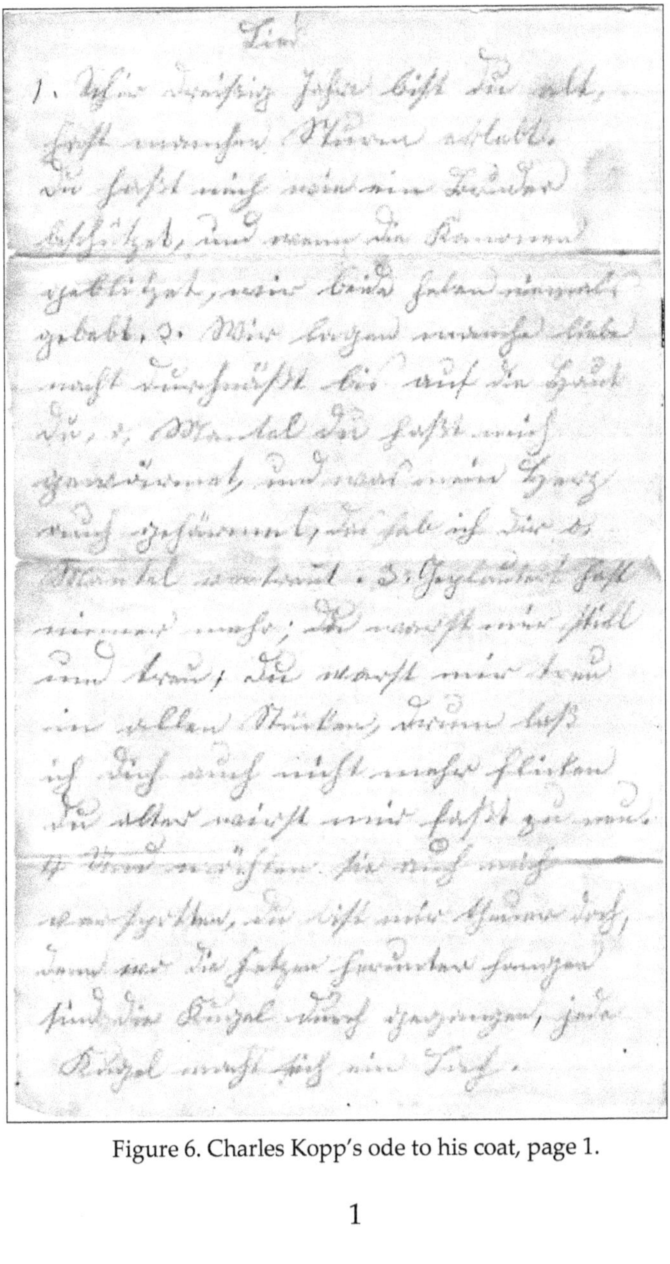

Charles J. Kopp's song

Figure 6. Charles Kopp's ode to his coat, page 1.

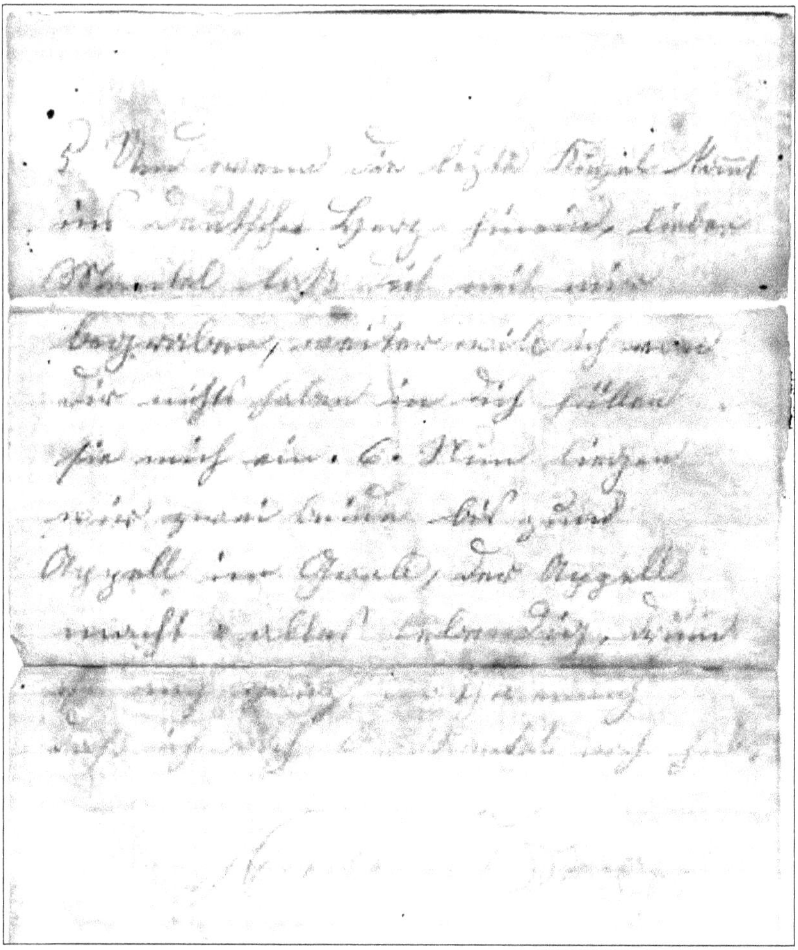

Figure 7. Charles Kopp's ode to his coat, page 2.

Lied	Song
1. Schier Dreißig Jahre bist du alt, hast manchen Sturm erlebt. Du haßt mich wie ein Bruder beschützet, und wenn die Kanonen geblitzet, wir beide haben niemals gebebt.	1. You're about thirty years old and have endured quite a few storms. You have protected me like a brother, and when the cannons fired, the two of us have never shuddered.
2. Wir lagen manche liebe nacht durchnäßt bis auf die Haut du, o, Mantel du haßt mich gewärmet, und was mein Herz auch gehärmet, das hab ich dir o, Mantel vertraut.	2. We lay quite some dear nights drenched to the skin—you, oh, coat you have warmed me, and all that harmed my heart I have entrusted to you, oh, coat.
3. Geplautert hast nimmer mehr; du warst mir still und treu; du warst mir treu in allen Stücken, drum laß ich dich auch nicht mehr flicken du alter wirst mir faßt zu neu.	3. You have never talked; you were always quiet and loyal to me; you were faithful in all aspects, that is why I will not have you mended; you, old pal, are becoming almost too new.
4. Und möchten sie auch mich verspotten, du bist mir theuer doch, denn wo die Fetzen herunter hangen sind die Kugel durch gegangen, jede Kugel macht sich ein Loch.	4. And if they mock me, to me you are precious nonetheless, because where tatters hang down, bullets have gone through, each bullet made a hole for itself.
5. Und wenn die lezte Kugel kommt ins deutsche Herz hinein, lieber Mantel laß dich mit mir begraben, weiter will ich von dir nichts haben in dich hüllen sie mich ein.	5. And when the last bullet comes, entering into the German heart, dear coat, let yourself be buried with me, nothing else do I ask of you, but that they unfold me into you.
6. Nun liegen wir zwei beide bis zum Appell im Grab, der Appell macht alles lebendig, drum ist auch ganz nothwendig daß ich dich o Mantel auch hab.	6. Now we both lie in the grave until roll call, roll call will bring everything to life, that is why it is so very important that I have you indeed, oh coat.
Charles Kopp	Charles Kopp

[DIARY OF A MISSOURI VOLUNTEER]

A MILITARY CAMPAIGN
IN MISSOURI AND ARKANSAS
FROM A FORMER OFFICER OF THE 15TH
MISSOURI INFANTRY (SWISS) REGIMENT[7]

IMAGES FROM LIFE IN THE
AMERICAN WAR

I.

Previous Events. The Southwest Army.
The Marching Order and Its Immediate Aftermath.

The summer of 1861, the first of the Civil War, did not go well for the Union troops in Missouri. In small divisions scattered throughout the territory, they found the enemy superior everywhere, and they were forced into retreat or defeat. Their largest army, under General Lyon, was defeated in the Battle of Wilson's Creek, close to Springfield. Lyon himself was killed, and his troops retreated hastily back to St. Louis. Almost the entire territory south of the Missouri River was now in the hands of the Rebels, and even northern Missouri was exposed

---

[7] This title was crossed out by the author and replaced by the following title: *Images from the Life in the American War.*

to their raids. The Rebel army consisted mostly of Missourians and was occasionally strengthened by troops from southern states. Their leader was the old Price—that is, price[8]—a clever, unrelenting general who was most popular and whose outer appearance, as well as mental aptitude and eloquence, awarded him a winning personality.

   The supreme commander of the Federal troops in the West, General Major Fremont, was meanwhile occupied with organizing an army out of the troops recruited from western states and from Missouri itself, and he finally led the entire military force into the field by the end of September. The individual army corps pushed down from the Missouri River in a southwestern direction, and they united close to Springfield, the capital of southwest Missouri. From there, Fremont wanted to force the enemy—who had retreated from us at every location while also concentrating into one force—to engage in a decisive battle between Springfield and the border of Arkansas. Then, however, he was relieved by a command from Washington, and his successor[9] immediately gave the order to retreat. One part of the army was sent to another battleground, and the rest, including our division, moved into winter quarters halfway between Springfield and St. Louis, near Rolla (the last station of the railroad leading to St. Louis), and henceforth became the "Army of the Southwest." The enemy had naturally followed us on foot and scattered within the territory we had given up; Price himself opened his headquarters in Springfield. The Army of the Southwest, however, lay for 2½ months, from mid-November until the end of January, partly in barracks and partly under tents, idly on the snow in Rolla—concerned more about the pitcher than the war, sharpening the tongue rather than the saber, and only

---

[9] Henry Wager Halleck (January 16, 1815–January 9, 1872)

thinking of drink and food, while thus, exposing the Missouri prize to General Price.¹⁰

At the beginning of January, Brigadier General Curtis was appointed the supreme commander of the Army of the Southwest. He was formerly a lawyer or politician with a face, and particularly his nose, glowingly red and the somewhat jovial expression of a genuine court bailiff or peace judge in the great wide West.¹¹ He was a man of great wealth, good family, influence, and—as he demonstrated later when he became military governor of Arkansas and, thus, of cotton—a lucky and astute businessman.

Figure 8. General Samuel R. Curtis. *Harper's Weekly*, March 8, 1862.

---

¹⁰ These German wordplays are partly rhymes and partly proverbial alliterations, and they demonstrate the author's poetic skills while expressing his frustration about the misguided military strategy: *mehr um den Krug als den Krieg, wetzte lieber den Schnabel als den Sabel, dachte nur an Trank und Speis, gab dem Price Missouri preis*. This passage also references the play *Wallenstein* by Friedrich Schiller, the classical German author and poet: "And the army lies here in Bohemia—while attending to the needs of the stomach, there is little quarrel."

¹¹ The author is probably referring to the famous literary character Adam, the village judge in Heinrich von Kleist's *Der Zerbrochene Krug*.

The new general greeted his army with a daily command, in which he announced that an arduous campaign through rough, uninviting, mountainous terrain lay ahead, and he ordered the troops to get prepared and to get rid of everything dispensable. We were easily able to guess what the mountainous terrain he alluded to was. We knew it only too well from our last retreat from Springfield, and now we were reminded again, vividly and with horror, of those wild environs, which still look as if only Indians and rabbits dwell there. [I had also never met more miserable and uneducated people than in this deserted region... We entered log-houses—since frame houses were a rarity here, and I do not recall having seen rock houses— whose inhabitants did not even recognize the silver coins we offered them as reimbursement for a meal consisting of cornbread, molasses, and ham.] We were also reminded of the rough, steep mountain paths and indescribable torture of animals, to which our poor mules had to suffer and to which quite a few had fallen victim.

> IMPORTANT FROM ROLLA.—A gentleman from Rolla last night conveys to us the important information that a column of 5,000 infantry were under orders yesterday to march westward from that point. The force is to be under the command of Gen. Osterhaus. The troops are composed of detachments from Sigel's and Asboth's divisions. It was thought that the Thirty-sixth Illinois and the Fourth Iowa would also be included. It is conjectured in military circles in Rolla that General Price has sent out his cavalry eastward from Springfield to hold the federal forces under Carr and Wright in check, while he will effect a retreat with his whole army to Arkansas.—*St. Louis Democrat*, 17*th*.

Figure 9. *Liberty Tribune*, January 24, 1862.

The impression this announcement of the highest warlord had caused amidst his legions resulted in many of our warriors, among them also officers, seeking to exempt themselves with or without permission, and hundreds of our soldiers pushed to see their doctors in order to be left behind in the hospitals or to be relieved from duty due to chronic illnesses or incurable diseases. Almost all of these afflictions, present for many years, had not hindered individuals from entering the service and remaining there as long as they could receive pay and live at the government's expense without great strain and danger, but when the arduous campaign was announced, they suddenly remembered. It was indeed incredible the kinds of ailments, and how many, had now come to light in our regiments: senile infirmity and partial blindness, the missing of fingers on the right hand and deformed feet, consumption and heart defects, old foot sores and bone fractures of all varieties and lengths—in short, it was an ample collection of splendid specimens of all those ailments that are expressly identified and defined in army regulations as to prohibit entry in the army.

Naturally, such people were discharged as unusable, but the following proves that a good number of those later applied to receive good pay again, just to be dismissed once more due to physical unfitness. There were plenty of applicants who engaged in this fraud and who helped other applicants avoid the mandatory physical examination. They were only interested in supplying a certain number of recruits to supplement their eligibility when, sooner or later, applying for an officer's patent. And it worked; ragged innkeepers or beer waiters, cobblers, and tailors, thus, became lieutenants and captains. Some benefited financially with the good pay of these positions and improved their financial standings, some even made a fortune, and everyone came out on top. The tailor helped the cripple to get pay, and the cripple helped the tailor to get an officer's salary. One good turn deserves another; that is the principle in business, and being a soldier had equally become a business.

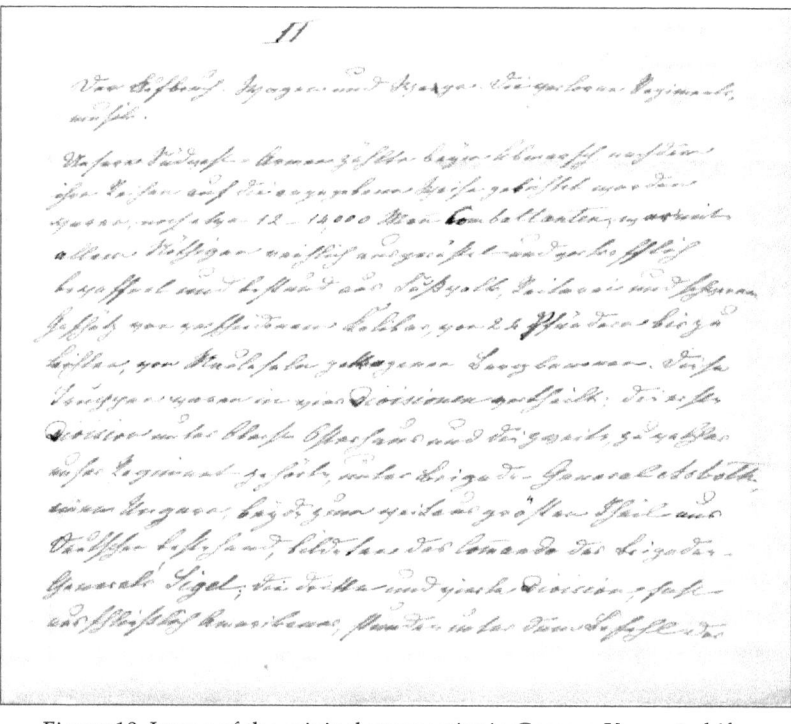

Figure 10. Image of the original manuscript in German Kurrentschift..

Rolla, February 1, 1862

II.
The Departure. Wagons and Trails.
The Lost Regiment Music.
[Gasconade River, February 2, 1862]

At the departure, our Army of the Southwest still accounted for about twelve thousand combatants after its ranks had been cleared in the indicated fashion. It was abundantly equipped with everything necessary, it was superbly armed, and it consisted of infantry, cavalry, and heavy artillery of various calibers: 24-pounders to lighter mountain howitzers[12] carried by mules. These troops were divided into four divisions: the First Division under Colonel Osterhaus and the Second, to which our regiment belonged, under Brigadier General Asboth, a Hungarian. The vast majority of both of these divisions consisted of Germans and formed the command of Brigadier General Sigel. The Third and Fourth Divisions, consisting

---

[12] The author uses the work "*bergkanone*," which is a mountain gun used where wheeled transport is not possible and is generally capable of being broken down into smaller loads. It is sometimes called a "pack gun" or "pack howitzer."

almost exclusively of Americans, stood under the command of Colonels Davis and Carr.

These divisions departed separately and at different times at the end of January and embarked on their marches on two nearly parallel roads. Our division was the last to receive marching orders. It still took eight entire days until it was executed, that is, until we had the required number of wagons and mules to transport our baggage, food, and munitions, [in spite of having left everything unessential behind and being considerably decimated—partly from discharging men from duty and partly from leaving behind many of the weak and sick at the Rolla hospital.]

In those days, it was still different than it would be two years later under Sherman and others, when the soldier would have to carry part of the small tents, including cooking gear, on top of his knapsack, and the officer would have to carry his luggage in a bag. We lived in the good times, in which old army regulations from before the war were still enacted for the Regular army for the long marches on the prairies of the West. Each company had one wagon that carried its large tents, munitions, cooking gear, and other company properties, as well as the luggage of officers: large suitcases, field beds, and even stoves. Furthermore, the staff officers had a wagon; the doctors had another, which carried the essentials for establishing a field hospital; and the quartermaster had a few wagons. Each of these heavy freight wagons was harnessed with four mules—strong, splendid animals the size of a midsize horse. One might imagine what a retinue of horses and songbirds[13] each regiment resembled and how cumbersome the movement of such a convoy had to be, especially considering the bad condition of American roads.

---

[13] This wordplay in German suggests that there were both clutter and chatter, or literally, "where there are horses there must also be siskins" (*zeisig*).

Much easier and quicker than transporting the essentials was leaving behind everything dispensable. All that was not privately owned, such as tents, stoves, and so forth, was just left scattered behind with the assumption that the chief of the quartermaster depot in Rolla (which was Major Sheridan, the one who should later become the famous general) would look after it and collect it. Since that was not happening quickly enough, and since left-behind soldiers and other helpful civilian neighbors busied themselves by assisting in the removal, they did without pay what thousands of soldiers with pay did to the property of the state.

It was on the morning of February 1, 1862, when our regiment departed at last. Leading us marched a dandy music band with partly silver instruments, and then came the regiment with its many officers—altogether hardly more than six hundred men. Directly behind them were two ambulance wagons, one of which transported the first casualties, two heavily inebriated officers: a major—a miller by profession—and a lieutenant—a barber. At the end of the entourage followed, under the cracking of whips and cursing of coachmen (all the soldiers of the regiment assigned to that position), the long convoy of highly stacked wagons and, on top, an occasional officer's lad—boys with gleaming prankster faces thereby enjoying the school of life. Also swaying on top of the wagons were laundresses and other female servants of all kinds of color—white, yellow, or black; however, like baggage, what was at all dispensable was left behind.

During the previous eight days, the heavens spared no effort with rain, snow, and frost to make us fear the worst about the impending march, and the first day already justified these fears completely. Not one hundred steps outside the area of our former campground, which we passed through, our first wagon got stuck in the mud, and very nearby, our whole train had come to a standstill because, then, a munitions wagon of the artillery had sunk so deeply that ten horses were pulling in vain to move it from its spot.

But an even deeper impression than that which our wagons had left on the road was that which the road had left on our musicians. In spite of their great affinity to the wet,[14] as is characteristic of all musicians, the wetness of their feet instilled such a shock about the beautifully anticipated—but now arduous—campaign that one musician after the other stayed behind. And when roll call was held in the evening, it turned out that the entire music band with their silver and tin instruments had vanished as a whole with all their belongings. When, after some time, we were able to read newspapers from St. Louis, we found an invitation to the honorable readership to attend the musical evening entertainment of the famously known music band of the "Swiss Regiment." For us, this gang had been lost for good, and we had to make do with our drummers and trumpeters. The former were boys from the ages of fifteen to seventeen who worked over the wooden drums quite courageously, and the latter were young men who did their best to produce ear-shattering cacophonies on tin pipes bent only by a single curve. Some American regiments had time-honored fife players instead of these so-called trumpeters, and when they would commence with an American or an Irish nationalistic march in unison with the wooden drums, it sounded just like the music to a bear's dance.

III.
Military Obedience. The First Camp.
A Log-House in Missouri.

We marched briskly forward through the snow and over the hilly country covered with brush. The goal of our first march was the place where the small creek, the Little Piney, flows into the mountainous stream, the Gasconade. When we were still

---

[14] This is a German wordplay referring to those who like to drink alcohol.

4½ miles (that is 1½ hours) away, however, a few officers declared that they did not intend to march any further until the wagons with tents and provisions had caught up with us. The colonel gave orders to continue the march, but to no avail! The number of dissenting officers increased, and their demand to stop here had become peremptory. And so the colonel's only choice was either to march on with a smaller number of abiders or—more democratically—to comply with the will of the majority and, thereby, disobey the order issued by the general after his own subordinates had disobeyed.

The good colonel gave in, and we stopped in order to wait for our train. But it did not appear, and thus, we were forced to camp on the field of a farm situated next to the road. Without having anything warm to eat, the troops spent the first night on the snow and exposed to an extremely frosty wind. A small number of us had the privilege of finding shelter and food in two log-houses. The farmer was a Union man—a genuine Missouri Union man—with whom we became acquainted well enough: quite curt in his speech, without any inclination to engage in a conversation about politics or war according to the American custom, and obviously very displeased with our visit. He charged us copiously for his coffee and bacon and even for permission to sleep on the floor of his hut—one-quarter of a dollar for each person. He was quite irritated when his impertinent bill was substantially reduced by the colonel for burnt fence rails and a few shot piglets. In America, each piece of farmed property is surrounded by a fence that consists of shorter and longer posts ("fence rails").[15]

His log-house was indeed the original dwelling of a small Missouri farmer: a simple room with two doors on opposing sides without locks and latches, but with a hole in the raw wood through which a hand could stretch out to pull open the tightly fitting, massive door. Naturally, it was without

---

[15] This sentence is a footnote in the original German narrative.

windows either but full of gaps and holes in the roof and walls—"a mosquito net," as it was called by one of our officers, who could not find enough words of displeasure about such unwholesomeness and laziness of an old settler owning 160 acres[16] of good land and having several grown sons. In even worse condition was the smaller log-house located in the back, the abode of one son with a young, pretty woman and several little ones.

Most of our officers lay stretched out in a semicircle on the floor of these cabins without padding or covers other than their coats and with their feet pointing to the fireplace, which—piled up of rocks—looked like a fortified turret full of firing slits built into the house. It was so large that, indeed, a pyre of enormous pieces of half or of entire tree trunks was ablaze inside. Its heat caused the boots of some of us to burn while the more distant upper body froze considerably.

The following morning, our quartermaster brought the pleasant news that our carts were still not moving from their spot. Thus, after freezing throughout the night, we also had to abstain from warming coffee and from food in general, apart from a few piglets that had been shot and roasted [and a few crackers, which a few of us luckily had left in our pockets.] To lift spirits within our pleasant situation even further, a severe blizzard arose, which lasted all day and into the night.

Finally, between two and three o'clock, our carts arrived, but prior to that, our general had returned to inquire about the cause of our absence and to command us to immediately commence marching. We had just enough time left to boil coffee in haste and to cover the remaining 4½ miles.

---

[16] The author uses the word *"juchart,"* which in Switzerland, generally referred to a measure of land that could be ploughed in the course of one day. Before becoming standardized, the acre referred to the same measure.

One can imagine how comfortable I felt in the evening of that day, finally laying stretched out on my cot in a warm tent, next to me a cup of tea with brandy, and using my case on which to enter the most recent experiences into my journal. I was without any worry other than how to avoid my feet touching the floor, which turned into a real mire after the heat of the stove had melted the snow. Belonging to the amenities of the officer's rank was a little stove, which sometimes, and with luck, was included as an accessory of the tent by the quartermaster and consisted of a cylinder made of sheet metal without a bottom but with a little door and a long straight pipe that peeked out of the tip of the tent.

Big Piney River, February 3, 1862

IV.
Over Mountain and Valley.
A Country Town in the West. Soldier's Logic.
[Big Piney River, February 4, 1862]

[While standing at a small fire to warm my feet, I used the time to briefly sketch the previous day's march until our carriages and artillery climbed a mountain next to our camp—the steepest mountain we had to ascend so far.] The next morning brought beautiful weather; the ground was covered with firm snow, and to that circumstance we gratefully attributed that, in spite of the steep, mountainous paths, our carts kept up with our pace. [If we still had the soft snow and slough of the day we departed from Rolla, it would have been quite impossible to overcome the steep heights and deep ravines that we traversed and that lay ahead of us. Even so, our march progressed slowly; nine miles was the entire distance covered that day.

At about two o'clock, we entered a small canyon at the sight of which a thought came to me involuntarily: how quickly a convoy like ours would perish here. With our back and both sides boxed-in by wooded heights, the canyon was barely wide enough for the road and a creek, which twisted over the rocky and shaggy ground. Still, one of these poor Missouri nomads (we soldiers call them "hoosiers"[17]) travailed down a steep descent separated from us by the creek and hidden by the shrubs, maneuvering a little cart with his few belongings.] We descended into a deep, narrow gorge and hit upon a tangled cluster of carts, cannons, foot soldiers, and cavalry, who all rushed to stride through a small river lying ahead of us, the Big Piney.

It was a part of our own division and a part of the First Division with whom we met there for the first time. The mass of people, however, was not nearly as large as the number of regiments represented there would have suggested. These were not anymore the complete regiments, nine hundred to one thousand men strong, which had marched with us last spring under the leadership of Fremont ["on to Springfield!"]

Weather, hardship, and particularly the gall fevers and typhus illnesses prevalent in this country had decimated the ranks enormously, even before they had seen the enemy. A single, small regiment from Illinois had buried about 170 men

Figure 11. General John C. Fremont (right) and General Franz Sigel (left). Photo courtesy of Dennis Hood.

---

[17] The original German text spells the word "huschers," which refers to "hoosiers." The origin of this word is uncertain, but it was likely used to refer to those who lived in the mountains or hills.

in the foreign country during the 2½ months we were stationed at Rolla. During the same time, our German division had only suffered two deaths per regiment. Here, we had the opportunity to see for ourselves how beneficial it is for our troops to live dispersed and exposed to air and cold in tents and how some people develop an almost superhuman appetite and become strong and fat. We also had the opportunity to see the condition of others who lived together in large barracks, which are much more disadvantageous to health and so easily become breeding grounds for epidemics.

[The impact of a river-crossing scene was more pleasant to a group that had weakened in number. Along with a truly picturesque image, which this scene awarded, it also offered a favorable impression. The spirits of troops that marched onward slowly, and often lonely, were newly invigorated by the general sentiments, and it was simultaneously strengthened by the consciousness of being part of a larger, well-organized throng.]

The Big Piney is neither deep nor ripping. The foot soldiers were taken across on the unloaded baggage carts. The cannons, however, were likely to be knocked over, especially those on heavily loaded carts. These strained the abused animals extensively until they had been trudged through the ice-cold water. Thus, this river crossing claimed the rest of the day.

At the other shore of the Big Piney, a wide valley basin spread out, bordered by high wooded mounds. [We made this our resting quarters for the rest of the day and night.] When we climbed the incline of this mountainous range the next morning, we stood at the summit of uncultivated, forested hills, which expanded as far as the eyes could see to both sides in front of us. The nearly complete absence of human dwellings and farmed land, the woods and meadows, the deep gorges and the gentle valley basins—which were phased out by similarly high wooded mounds—gave this region the image that an Indian tribe still roamed its hunting grounds. [The imagination certainly did not know what to do with us, the advancing United States soldiers, in this miserable state of Missouri!]

Waynesville, February 4, 1862

[Waynesville, February 5, 1862]

[Here, I was writing from on top of a horse. Our wagons had been slowed by the soft and deeply rutted ground; one wagon became stuck only five minutes after our departure. We established our camp about two miles outside Waynesville. A pleasant march led us there, of which we had only a few even during the mild season. After we had ascended the mountain range bordering the Big Piney, the fire of a new, large frame house—a spectacle to which we meanwhile became accustomed—sent smoke after us.] Only late in the afternoon the road declined again, and we entered a deep valley basin.

Here lay the little town of Waynesville, the seat of the county and the type of little country town of the American West. At the center was the courthouse, the only stone building in town, surrounded by wide, free space, which seemed to suggest how many more houses could still find room in order to turn Waynesville into a city. Dispersed in a large area stood about three modestly sized frame houses—that means wooden houses of one or two stories, of which the inner walls and halls are plastered and the outside walls are painted white—and furthermore, a full dozen boarded shacks ("shanties") and log-houses. I was unable to discover a church, which was to my great astonishment since I would have expected at least three churches and at least as many religious congregations in an American settlement of two dozen houses.

There were a small number of streets—almost without any houses, of course—all parallel in two rows that crossed in right angles. In part, these streets carried names already. It was certain, however, that these arranged squares had been divided carefully into building lots that were possessed by those with title deeds in hopes that they will be a source of money when Waynesville becomes a large city. This is the course of how cities are founded in this region, often based on stocks of companies in the Far East. First, the streets are surveyed, and the lots are determined. Then, the "child" is named, often by some famous person or by an antediluvian city, such as Memphis or Utica, and this name is, from now on, drawn into the maps. And now the speculation begins: The town is announced and praised in the major papers of the country, lots are put up for sale, they are bought, the prices are driven up, and the lots are sold again and become the main subject of American speculation. A person in the East, anticipating much from the future of his property ownership in the backwoods of Missouri or Iowa, puts great hopes in such building lots of a western town. From year to year, he expects to hear that this region will suddenly bloom and that he will become a rich landowner and landlord. For the present, however, his land serves only as a pasture for cows and geese, and it brings only costs and yearly taxes for the city, county, state, and country. If he impatiently inquires with an inhabitant of Waynesville—or whatever the name of the young town is—for information, he will hear this assurance: "The town has a future and a great future at that. It will blossom as soon as there is a railroad or a train of immigrants heading here to populate the region." All inhabitants of such a place are doused with such a conviction, and all are eager to persuade any stranger who travels to this region by chance to settle down.

We were the only ones they did not hold back; from us, almost all people in Waynesville fled. [There appeared more houses present than inhabitants. Next to a few old Negro women and dogs, we could see only a few. During a rest of fifteen minutes, most officers were concerned about finding lunch, or at least a cup of coffee. With a friend,] I used the short stop in this little town to inspect the courthouse. All doors were unlocked or smashed in, nobody was found on the lower level, the archives had been emptied, and generally, almost everything was removed. In one of the rooms, however, I still found the high, long shelves filled with those unavoidable thick tombs bound in yellow calf's leather, which constitute the basics of the American local government. These were books according to which justice was exercised, and without which people would not know what is just. There were so many (and are so many even in the smallest, most remote place of the United States), specific and particular for each state, that it is possible there are more lawyers in America than there are priests in Italy.[18] I looked at these long shelves with disgust, and then, I had to ask myself whether in this whole county there might be as many log-houses as there are yellow leather books that represent the law to these backwoodsmen. [In spite of my natural antipathy against such leather books, I searched through these archives with such eagerness that a spectator might have guessed I was looking for papers endangering the state or for a census of local citizens who paid the most taxes and fed the most niggers.]

On the upper floor, everything had been emptied as well. I did, however, encounter an unexpected group of artillery men

---

[18] This is based on a German saying that compares plentitude to the amount of clerics in Italy.

who had been left behind by their battery and did not know where it went. Now, they intended to look for it at a leisurely pace. They rested here, stretched out on the floor around a lit fireplace, and they spent their time issuing deeds to each other according to the files found in the archive. Each would get so many acres of land in Pulaski County. Disappointed, I left the courthouse. My inspection was aimed at finding a map of Missouri, but in vain! The good citizens of Waynesville had brought everything somewhat valuable to safety; nothing had remained but the bare walls and those leather books, and they were safe.

We opened our overnight camp about two miles further down the road. On the way there, a secessionist had the misfortune of having his farm standing there; he paid for that with his entire supply of oat, corn, poultry, and hay[, which was transported with great efficiency from his barn into the camps of our troops.] That this man was a secessionist would have been a mystery to everyone except to soldiers. A soldier's logic, however, deduces in such cases simply and concisely: Since the man owns something, he must be a secessionist, and one has to take what he has. This conclusion is perfectly correct, since in the Southern army, the very same logic applied, and the final result was that when both armies passed by, no one was left with anything.

[A humongous rooster also originated from that barn, but one of my men's bloodthirstiness spilled over to secessionist fowl. I probably should have delivered it back to its master; however, since darkness had already ensued, I had no choice but to digest the criminal evidence after sentencing it to death by ax and dagger for the purpose of satisfying my hungry stomach. A revengeful fate, however, punished me for such acquisition of foreign possession by destroying all beautiful hopes for a delicate dinner. It might have been my inexperience in cooking, or it might have been the age of the creature or its rebellious origin, but the roast was so tough that I could not find any more taste in it than with the leather books at the courthouse.]

V.
Spotless Discipline. War Whinings.

Shortly before departure on the next morning, a scene unfolded in our regiment that would have made the hair of officers in the Regular army stand on end.[19] The colonel had issued a command to a captain, and the captain had flatly refused to obey it. Then, the colonel rode to the captain and engaged in a discussion. The captain, however, attacked the colonel with a wrath-glowing face and clenched fists and overwhelmed him with an unending barrage of curses, swearwords, and scornful laughter. All the time, he was screaming so loud that half of the regiment gathered, and the captain swung his fists so menacingly that everyone expected a fight to ensue. The colonel, however, remained calm and restrained himself more to a mental resistance. This only led to the most provoking and derogatory swearwords known in the American-English language. Especially frequently, the expressions "deceiver," "traitor," and "liar" were dropped—all words that in civil life among Americans in the North would immediately result in a punch; in the South, in a revolver shot. All these niceties flew in eloquent English out of the big mouth of the captain, since the German in America will always use English when he curses; it seems this language is more suited for that.

The demeanor of the captain was even more daring since he knew he was not alone in this fight. There were a few regiments in our volunteer army whose officers busied their minds with forming parties that fought with every conceivable

---

[19] The equivalent German idiom literally translates to "let hair stand up like a mountain."

conspiracy in an attempt to unsettle each other. Frequently, a lieutenant colonel would stand at the head of the subversive party, and the common conclusion was that a number of officers had to bite the dust. That doesn't mean they were falling victim in a duel (duels were not only against the law, but also they were violating the ethics of the officers' corps); they were simply relieved of their duty. Such a quarrel was conducted with the greatest passion and eagerness in our regiment by repeated performances, which shows contempt to all conduct and discipline. That day's performance ended with having the sword removed from the captain and sentencing him to ride behind the regiment from then on; this had the advantage that he could sit on a horse. At the earliest opportunity, he should have faced a war tribunal, but since there had been neither opportunity nor motivation for that, the captain did receive his sword and command back after a certain period of time, and he then became, again, the old officer and gentleman.

Lebanon, February 6, 1862

[Lebanon, February 6, 1862]

Two days of marching led us through mountainous terrain, lower and more populated than the one traversed before, to the little town of Lebanon, where we met up with the rest of the entire army. Rain and melting weather had melted the snow, and a warm spring sun sent its reviving rays down to us. At the campground, we were greeted by a gentle, sunny meadow traversed by a creek, adorned by small groups of trees, and covered with this grass from which our white, pointed tents peaked like sugar hats. [At the same location, on the other side of the road, lay the First Division. This was the most pleasant camp we had ever had, and in the near distance, one could see the roofs of Lebanon. We prepared ourselves for a longer stay, and this break was quite welcome. We had two days of cumbersome marching, which led us from Waynesville to here. The first one took us over mountainous terrain to the Gasconade at dusk. When we crossed the river and put up our tents on the steep banks, a massive rain came over us, which lasted the entire night and transformed the campground and roads into mire. In addition, when we departed early in the morning, a severe cold ensued, the kind of which often follows rain in higher regions. The following march was the most arduous we had to face. I had the miserable choice of either walking through knee-high dirt, snow, and water, or having my feet frozen stiff while sitting on my horse. I chose the latter but was quite happy to find a log-house at the side of the road after two hours. A cozy warmth from the fireplace revived my frozen limbs. An hour passed with conversation and smoking while it started to get warmer outside, and I followed our regiment in a quick trot. The farmer who lived in the log-house was a Union man and signaled that by a little flag that hung in front of his door. For that reason, a cavalrist was standing guard in front of his farm to protect him from close confrontation with the passing Union troops. Therefore, only a few of our officers asked the man for permission to sit at his fireplace. Among those was an elderly man with bright, comprehending eyes and the sharply defined physiognomy of a Yankee. Talkative, like everyone else, he started to chat with me right away. He was from Ohio and not a soldier, although he carried a blue soldier's coat. He was quite happy not to be a soldier, but he had a son in the Second Ohio Battery, which was part of our division. His son lay ill with consumption in the hospital in Rolla, and the military doctor had given up on him. My neighbor came to Missouri to see his son, and in order to ask for his release from duty, he accompanied us to Lebanon.

When I asked him how he liked Missouri, he shook his head with a smile and said that it was the most miserable land he had seen. He had been here for almost four weeks, but he would be most relieved when he could return to his family in Ohio. How beautiful it was at Lake Erie where he lived!

"Don't you agree that is the most beautiful place in the world?" asked my other neighbor from Switzerland.

"Most certainly it is," answered the American with naïve self-assurance, and to support his statement, he began to paint an enthusiastic image of his picturesque home at Lake Erie.

The farmer's wife followed this narrative with a melancholic gaze. She sat by their children in the room with us. When we asked her how they would earn their keep in this country and by what means they would live presently, her eyes filled with tears, and she gave us the following information: Formerly, they had made a good and plentiful living. They had grown wheat and grain and transported it for twenty-five miles to a mill, or they kept some in stock and sold it to traveling tradesmen. They also had horses, cattle, and pigs. For raw pork, they could get five cents per pound last year, and for one pair of oxen, they could get sixty to seventy dollars. Now, however, everything had changed. Pork is worth only 2½ cents, a pair of oxen is worth no more than twenty-five to thirty dollars, and one is fortunate to sell anything at all. They would no longer know from what to live had they not hidden away many things. The secessionists, fifteen hundred of which had camped in their vicinity, had taken everything they could find away from them. Even the Union troops who had passed by several times had taken much away. For some things they had received notes from the government, but often that was neglected. At least they could regard themselves fortunate in comparison to many other Union people in the neighborhood; everything had been taken away from them, and now they lived in utter despair.

We listened intently to this lady's descriptions; we knew that she was speaking the truth. We had been part of the annexed Union army, which—after giving up and clearing southwest Missouri—was followed by a long train of fleeing Union people. They had accepted the humanitarian offer from Sigel to follow under his protection and find a new homestead across the Mississippi in peaceful, fertile Illinois. They did this without means and in the middle of winter, while their house and home with all their possessions was left behind to the enemy in pursuit. Since then, during our stay in Rolla, we had the opportunity to see hundreds of such refugees who had hurried to get to the outermost railway station of the Southwest.

Being reminded of this misery by the narrative of the Missouri farmer's wife, I addressed the man from Ohio once more (as I was ready to get up), from whom the same war had taken the health and, soon, also the life of a child.

"What do you think about the war in Missouri?" I asked him.

"I don't understand how the government could spend so much money for this dejected Missouri," was the Yankee's answer.]

[During the Present Campaign (Continuation)]

Lebanon, Continued

[Benton County, Arkansas, February 20, 1862]

[Fourteen days passed since my last lines, which described the crusade across Missouri. (One need only ask the first Missourian whether it wasn't a campaign that caused crucifixes plentifully.[20]) Since then, we accomplished our next task: that of clearing Missouri of enemy troops. These lines were written already from the soil of Arkansas.

It was a pleasant rest, the days granted to us in Lebanon.] We rummaged about, cooked, and barbequed, as is customary on summer holidays at home. Our boys roamed the area in all directions with their guns, "hunting," they claimed, but the original settlers of our meadow, a good amount of little rabbits that had dispersed at our arrival[—similar to the real Missourian "hoosiers," who fled the area upon our arrival—] resembled

---

[20] This is wordplay on the German word for crusade, "*Kreuzzug,*" which means "campaign of the cross."

only a small contribution to our table. The real plunder consisted of pigs, sheep, and poultry of all kind, which wandered the woods where they had been driven for safety or which were caught and shot within the yards and in front of the eyes of their owners [no matter how much women cried and men insisted they were Union people. This was always a very dubious claim, especially when a half-fearsome and half-grinning face of a ragged Negro woman peaks out of one of the doors. The owners declared with an insincere anger that this was the very last animal they owned, and they would not know how to feed themselves and their family when their last possession was taken away. The latter declaration sounded a little more credible because we sometimes wondered about still finding so much in this region, which had been ravaged by war for such a long time.]

The soldier has no compassionate heart, not even for the whining of such a poor people as those we encountered in Missouri—a people who labors hard for bread and a wooden hut and for a pitiful life in the wilderness. Their only wealth seems to lie in a large blessing of children. As soon as a rabbit shrieked or a sheep bleated, avarice awoke in the soldier, and once it is awoken, the soldier knows no limits. He not only took what he needed[(that would be quite excusable)], but even things for which he had no use, and what he could not carry off often fell prey to his whim of destruction. Still etched in my memory of our last campaign are the famished appearances of two men at the grave of their belongings: a farmer whose plentiful sheep herd was blown to pieces and now covered the prairie, butchered by a troop of giddy cavalrists, and a weeping shoemaker (a German Union man) whose shoemaking tools—the only source of income for his family—had been taken from him by a German soldier without mercy before his eyes. The Southern troops were less inclined to destroy and ransack compared to ours for the good reason that this was the land of their homes, but they dealt much more mercilessly with all those they deemed to be friends of the North and supporters of the rightful government. The previous fall, a long trek of such Union people had followed the humanitarian command of Sigel and fled to Rolla under the protection of our army. During our stay there, we had enough opportunity to see these poor refugees who had been driven from house and farm in the midst of the cold winter. They hurried to this furthermost railway station with their few belongings in order to be brought from here across the Mississippi to start a new home in peaceful and fertile Illinois, while their old home was exposed to the vengeance of a ruthless enemy.[21]

[It is a peculiar sight to see a dead town. On our march through Missouri, every dwelling offered more or less such a sight, but none more than Lebanon. Lebanon—the outermost town held by the enemy in the direction of Rolla—is a town whose courts had ordered the forces to fight battle with us.]

Figure 12. Lebanon, Missouri, 1860s.
Photo courtesy of LegendsOfAmerica.com.

The little town of Lebanon, aside from its business streets, resembled a pile of irregularly dispersed houses over a stretch of rough plateau. Upon our arrival, it appeared as if the enemy

---

[21] Because the author described the refugees fleeing under General Sigel in different places in both of his narratives, the description is repeated in the combined account.

cavalry had turned the ground with the houses on its head and shaken it. All dwellings stood completely empty; inhabitants in this Lebanon were as scarce as cedars. [Otherwise, Lebanon might have accounted for eight hundred to a thousand inhabitants.

I tried to locate a local family to find out more about the enemy and about their own fate during the latest period of war, but wherever I peeked into a house all the way down Main Street, I found cavalrists everywhere.] Our cavalrists made themselves comfortable in the smaller houses, and in the few larger ones—stately looking dwellings of the earlier aristocracy—the generals opened their quarters. [They were the new inhabitants of the stores and offices, and they smoked or chatted while sitting around the stove or lying stretched out on the counter. On the shelves formerly holding wares and goods were scattered sabers, horse brushes, and other things, and in the adjoining rooms or supplementary buildings, horses had found their stables. In the yards or between the houses, there was an occasional officer's tent, and hanging along the fences for drying were freshly stropped sheepskins. Had it been a custom that American towns choose a coat of arms insignia, Lebanon could not have made a better choice than to set such a stropped sheepskin into their coat of arms. I directed my inquisitive walk toward a pretty country house at the end of the town and asked the cavalrist stationed in front of it about the inhabitant.

"General Sigel lives here," was the answer, and when I pointed to a second house, he said, "That is the headquarters of General Curtis."[22]

---

[22] The next paragraph is crossed out. It seems to contain a continuation of the dialogue between the author and the guard. The last three lines have also been crossed out but are legible. They read, "'Alright, thanks for the information,' I interrupted him and moved away from my companion with an indifferent expression, as hard

On our way home, we finally had the luck of finding a family of citizens. It consisted of a woman with a few children, who had shared two rooms of their house with a few cavalry officers. We sat down next to the woman at the fireplace and tried to get some information out of her, but we had only little success. We asked whether she could still make a living and how, what may have happened to the other inhabitants of Lebanon, and whether the secessionists who had been stationed here were Missourians or Southern troops. To all questions the same stereotypical answer followed: "I don't know." It was the same answer that we always received—with few exceptions—whenever we asked similar questions to Missourians. From a boy standing by, all we could find out was that about eighteen days ago the enemy troops had left Lebanon, they consisted of only eight hundred riders, they had been housed by friendly families, and no one had complained about their presence. When we asked the woman about her husband, she said that he was with the Northern army. Then, we knew enough. On our last campaign to Springfield, whenever we asked about the men, we were always told, "They are with General Sigel." At that time, we had marched separately from Sigel's division.]

Figure 13. General Franz Sigel shown here in a colonel's uniform. Photo courtesy of Dennis Hood.

---

as it was to keep from laughing—my companion was our field chaplain."

Marshfield, February 11, 1862

VI.
In Front of the Enemy. The First Shots.

On the morning of [Monday,] February 10, the Southwest army departed from Lebanon after it had established a quartermaster depot and field hospital there. On two separate roads, it moved toward Springfield. [The First and Second Divisions under Sigel's command (Curtis was commander in chief of the entire army) marched together; the Third and Fourth Divisions marched under Jefferson Davis from Indiana on another route in order to meet us again in Springfield.] The mild spring sun made us believe that wind and cold had been left behind for good the closer we moved toward the sunny South. Unburdened and cheerful, like hikers in the month of May, we marched across the hedged hills. A reasonably good road took us, by the evening of the second day, to the little town of Marshfield. Just that morning, before our arrival, the outposts of the enemy had stood there, and from there to the border of Arkansas, we expected to encounter them any day.

 A lively jumble of people and wagons characterized the departure of both Sigel's divisions on the following morning, and it took some time until the knot came untangled and the troops with their wagons started moving.

"Marshfield has never seen so many people at one time," a citizen remarked as he passed by with a forced smile on his face, while in secret he sent a curse after us as he observed the smoking ruins of a few houses that had been burnt during the delayed departure and as he looked through the broken windows of many abandoned dwellings, in which all that was left behind had been smashed. [When we were already in formation for the departure, our general came riding to the front and read the victory message from Fort Henry. A cheerful "hurrah" came as a response, and with the same victorious confidence, we marched toward the enemy just as we formerly did under Fremont.]

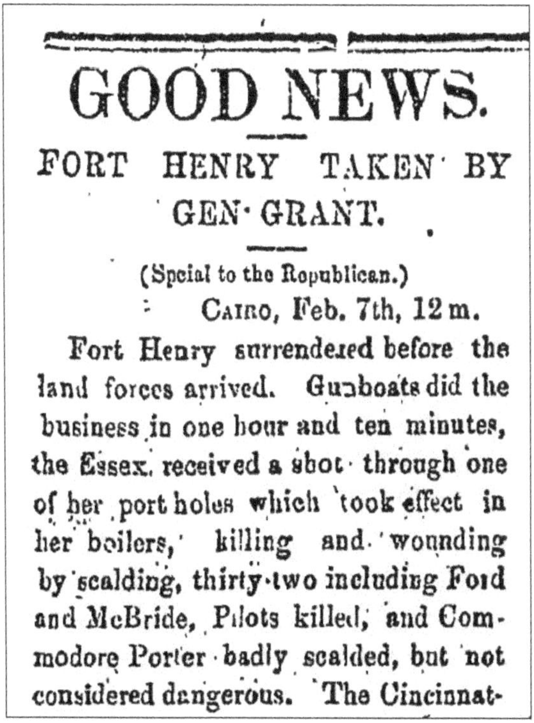

GOOD NEWS.

FORT HENRY TAKEN BY GEN· GRANT.

(Spcial to the Republican.)

CAIRO, Feb. 7th, 12 m.

Fort Henry surrendered before the land forces arrived. Gunboats did the business in one hour and ten minutes, the Essex received a shot through one of her port holes which took effect in her boilers, killing and wounding by scalding, thirty-two including Ford and McBride, Pilots killed; and Commodore Porter badly scalded, but not considered dangerous. The Cincinnat-

Figure 14. *Rolla Express*, February 10, 1862.

The hilly country in front of us started to look more savage, and in the afternoon, we entered a real wooded mountain range with steep declines and gorges. The road was rough and deeply rutted by the heavy artillery pieces, and the ground was soft and often so muddy that our walking folks had to find a path in the fields or through the forest. [In addition, the train of Sigel's division had at first preceded us until we passed it, frustrated by the many lengthy delays.] Thus, the march turned into a most cumbersome one; wagons got stuck all too soon, and they had to be pulled out again by men and by cattle under incredible cursing and beating. When they collapsed, they were dragged aside and the wagons were unloaded.

The further we moved on, the greater became the suspense with which we anticipated an explosion of gunfire, which would announce an encounter with the enemy. On such days, an obvious change could be observed among the troops. Instead of dispersing to the right and left or staying behind the convoy and moving on singing, chatting, or joking, they all stayed nicely together and walked quietly along the path, concentrated only on keeping their guns ready. It was about four o'clock in the afternoon, and we had just traversed a broad, wooded mountain slope when an upcoming fog and some sinister, black clouds emerged in front of us to darken the setting sun. As we got closer, a steadily increasing heat, a burning smell, and a loud crackling and rustling told us the forest had caught on fire. We rushed through the smoke, which limited our visibility to no more than two steps and severely hurt our eyes so that we could hardly open them. We moved through unbearable heat in order to cover the distance where—in a circumference of one mile on both sides of the road—the flames had spread rapidly. The wind had pushed the flames over dry leaves and grass and on to lower trees and bushes, of which these woods consist; they were gliding lightly and quickly, like squirrels, and jumping from one branch to the next.

During the day, we had already passed two forest fires. During the second one, a little farmer—equally fearful of us as he was of the flames—emerged as he tried to dig a long trench in order to draw a boundary to keep the fire off his nearby farm. [The last fire was the most formidable; the originators could only have been soldiers from Sigel's division, who had carelessly allowed this wicked joke without regard for their following comrades and their hurting eyes.]

At dusk, we reached a long gorge that crossed our way. Our division was supposed to rest here this night, and Sigel's division would move on a bit further. Since our wagons had stayed far behind, putting up the camp took little time. Each man found his supper in his own haversack, provided anything was left there, and he prepared his sleeping quarters on the rocky ground with collected leaves. Not long after lying down on our hard beds, we were jolted by three cannon shots in quick succession and the whirling of our drums calling us to formation. With a truly jubilant cheer, our guys jumped to the guns, and sprightly and undauntedly, they picked up the march again as if they had just rested and recovered from a long sleep. We had not covered a mile's distance, however, when the counter-order was issued commanding us to return to our beds made of leaves; only three companies that had to serve duty as outposts stayed behind.

After a short rest, we assembled again at around 4 AM. The knapsacks were thrown together [and left behind with a watch]; each of our soldiers had only his haversack and a blanket hanging over the shoulder. It was still night, but the sinking moon, whose direction we followed, dimly lit our path over the wooded mountain range. A frosty chill pushed us quickly forward. We had covered about four miles when we saw a lot of fading fires and various heaps of knapsacks, drums, and instruments left at the side of the road, indicating to us where the First Division, which had departed, had its night camp. It was here where the outpost of the enemy had greeted our front troops—a cavalry unit—with a few gunshots, and then, they were chased away by those three cannon shots from our side while leaving behind a few dead and wounded. Soon we received news (which was less unexpected than it was unwelcome) from a few returning equestrians that the entire army of the enemy had cleared Springfield and was in full retreat. Thus, we marched into Springfield the following morning without drawing our swords. Our division marched into Springfield for the second time, Sigel's for the third time. [On November 13, we had turned our backs on the enemy, and on February 13, we entered again, exactly three months later.]

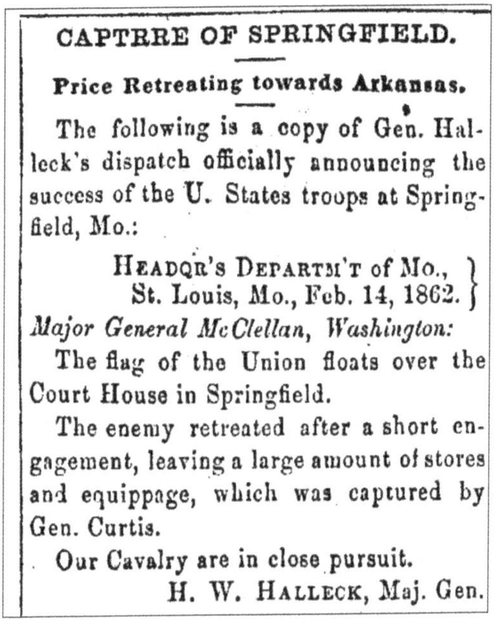

CAPTRRE OF SPRINGFIELD.

Price Retreating towards Arkansas.

The following is a copy of Gen. Halleck's dispatch officially announcing the success of the U. States troops at Springfield, Mo.:

HEADQR'S DEPARTM'T of Mo., }
St. Louis, Mo., Feb. 14, 1862. }

Major General McClellan, Washington:

The flag of the Union floats over the Court House in Springfield.

The enemy retreated after a short engagement, leaving a large amount of stores and equippage, which was captured by Gen. Curtis.

Our Cavalry are in close pursuit.

H. W. HALLECK, Maj. Gen.

Figure 15. *Liberty Tribune*, February 21, 1862.

Springfield, February 13, 1862

VII.
Entry into the Main Quarters of the Enemy.
Burning and Plundering.

Springfield, the capital of southwest Missouri, is a pretty and friendly little town with quite a few stately frame houses and a few large brick houses. It is situated on a hill and bordered on one side by a sloping meadow. [Four country roads meet in right angles on the squared marketplace, at the center of which stood the old courthouse that burnt down during our first entry. No further damage was caused, and the cause of the fire remains unknown. Springfield has, thus, gained a wide, spacious area, at the side of which the nearly completed new courthouse, a brick building, now stands.]

Just like our first entry the previous spring, the yellow hospital flag still waved on top of the courthouse, which marked it to both armies as a hospital [and which had protected the assistant doctor who was left behind last fall to take care of the wounded of Wilson's Creek. The same flag had designated another large brick house as the hospital for patients or wounded secessionists who were left behind. Before our retreat, all of our invalids had been removed. This time, we found the new courthouse to be the hospital of the secessionists.]

Figure 16. Springfield, Missouri. *Harper's Weekly*, November 20, 1861.

Thus, this yellow flag survived the other two flags in Springfield and in almost all of southern Missouri. That yellow flag indicates human misery, the neutral ground, where the sharp hook cuts as coldly and mercilessly into the flesh of the friend as well as the foe. Indeed, it was human misery that each of the enemy brothers had left behind—human misery that was expressed on the faces of the few inhabitants whom we were made aware on the streets of Springfield.

A physiognomist would have found abundant samples to interpret from the diverse facial features. They were so secretive and, yet, so expressive about the pouring out of their hearts' emotions. They had curiosity, the heritage of the American, and astonishment about whether it is possible that we had indeed re-entered this square, which we had given up to the enemy for three months. Occasionally, they had an unfortunate smile—unfortunate because it was a forced and, therefore, a futile expression of joy. Their basic features, however, dominated all the others: fear and terror—these spoke loudly from the faces of those few people who presented themselves fearfully in front of a few houses or who passed by quietly. These people begged for mercy with their lamenting or friendly gestures and words—today from us, yesterday from the enemy—and pleaded for us not to take their meager possessions, which were too small to leave behind and flee.

Springfield probably accounted for six thousand inhabitants. Then, however, it was almost abandoned. [Springfield was already an abandoned place when we first saw it in the fall of the year before, and it appeared even more abandoned that day. On the road on which we entered, there was a field of ragged trees close to the rows of houses, which immediately revealed itself to be the campground of a cavalry unit. Nicely hollowed-out logs indicated the great care the horsemen took for their horses. A good amount of grain scattered in heaps, a few large iron kettles, and other equipment implied that a departure had taken place not long ago.] Many houses and barns on this road stood empty and open; their floors had been layered with straw. Apparently, troops had slept there, and in all probability, these dwellings had belonged to Union folk who had fled. Many other houses— among which were splendid little frame houses supplied with pretty gardens and Negro dwellings that were located at some distance to both sides in the back—also seemed unoccupied, or at least no one was visible. They were, however, locked up and obviously untouched from any ill-intended hand. These houses were probably interpreted to belong to sympathizers of the South.

Without any preceding announcement, we moved through the city and out of it on the other side. On the square, we met a great number of prisoners. Without weapons or any war insignia, they looked just like ordinary farmers' boys. Here, we left a company behind as a guard; their effectiveness, however, was severely put to question, as following incidents will show. [We passed a large, single-story house, which suddenly awakened quite a few memories of Springfield—memories that generated a vivid image in front of the soul. This place was the former headquarters of Fremont.

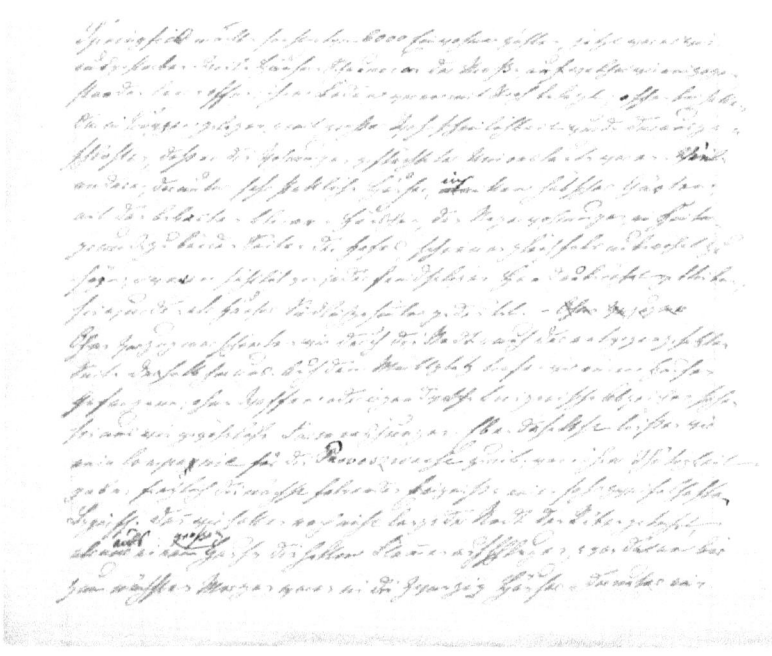

Figure 17. Image of the original manuscript in German Kurrentschrift.

What a colorful painting of life in war this house and its environment had once offered. I am never more vividly reminded of Wallenstein's[23] quarters than by this image. Many warriors of all parts of the army met and mingled. There were troops from mostly western states, from Ohio to Nebraska, and even a company of mounted Indians that Lane[24] had brought from Kansas: tall, agile figures with dark-skinned faces, long hair, and pointed hats; from afar they looked like Calabrians.[25]

Figure 18. General Jim Lane. *Harper's Weekly*, November 23, 1861.

There were also a good number of old European officers from all over the old continent, especially from the German and the Hungarian Revolution; a few young Italians of Garibaldi's

---

[23] Wallenstein is a famous general, mythologized in literature and folklore.
[24] James "Jim" Henry Lane (June 22, 1814–July 11, 1866)
[25] Calabria was a district of ancient Italy.

Southern army; and who must not be forgotten, the many old German soldiers and sergeants who rode as cavalrists and artillerists with ease and pride in the saddle that had been missed for so long. Quartered on the other side of the street were Fremont's personal guards: neat, slim, youthful equestrians. They had a right to be proud; they were the only men of the entire large army, who—by their daring riding skills—had the privilege to prove to the enemy and, even more so, to the friendly army in the East and to the rest of the world what kind of spirit had guided the Western army and what it was capable of doing.

However, the gods in the white Mount Olympus had other intentions. Our Wallenstein had been taken from us. Another general—an educated man from West Point[26]—came with a fateful letter in his pocket. He was too late, according to Fremont's plan, whereby he should have arrived a few days earlier in order to march against the enemy with the other divisions and, thus, strike the decisive blow. That man, however, still came too soon for us. We would have preferred to fight without him rather than retreat with him. It is difficult to imagine the complete reversal that the events of a few days could have on our troops. Shortly after our arrival in Springfield, a general marching order was issued around midnight. Knapsacks, tents, and all baggage were left behind, and "March ahead!" was the order. The hour of the daily-anticipated battle seemed to have come. The eagerness to fight and the confidence of victory, which shone from all faces, should have been witnessed. It seemed impossible to mishandle our weapons or even to think about a misstep. Whoever walked through the rows of tents and listened to the chatter of the soldiers encountered only jubilation and determination, not one word or face that showed fear. One or two evenings later, one could find the same groups standing around their fires; their speeches were

---

[26] Henry Wager Halleck (January 16, 1815–January 9, 1872)

becoming even louder and more heated, but indignation, disappointment, and helplessness were expressed. Even more disturbed, and possibly even more undecided, were the officers. An enormously depressed mood—just like the murky, hot, sultry air of a thunderstorm—had suddenly befallen their minds. "The spirit went to hell—only obedience remained."[27]

What followed is well-known. Only Sigel's division was sent to confront the enemy, who by now had time enough to retreat slowly, while all the other divisions departed in hasty retreat, leaving behind only our German division in Springfield. Sigel and ourselves at last found our way back to Rolla and the railroad, which could have, at best, taken us back to St. Louis. Last fall, we had confidently hoped that by Christmas we would have the enemy in front of us in warm Dixieland, leaving winter and cold behind us. Instead, we had been lying inactively for almost three months and were far removed from the enemy, safely in Rolla on the snow.

Again, I was reminded of Wallenstein's quarters, but this time about the Capucin's sermon:[28] "And the army lies here in Bohemia; while attending to the needs of the stomach, there is little quarrel," or as I had to alter the line involuntarily: "Only thinking of drink and food, while exposing the Missouri prize to General Price."[29]

One must forgive me for this deviation! I just had to air my discontent within the innocent lines of my diary. With soldiers' more hardened mentalities, such discontent might have

---

[27] This appears to be a quote from Friedrich Schiller's drama *Wallenstein*.

[28] This is a famous sequence in the play *Wallenstein*.

[29] The author attempts a German wordplay in which the words for "expose" (*preis geben*) and "Price" (*Preis*) can be rhymed.

assisted in fanning the fires—starting just at midday until the next morning when we marched in—that had destroyed into ashes some of the most beautiful houses of the unfortunate town of Springfield. Even Fremont's former quarters had fallen prey to this fate, and some who had been left unaffected by the fire were angered by the falling of this monument at a time when our warriors' spirits had blazed up high, but without destroying one home in Springfield.]

It was not long after we had passed through the city when one of the large houses was engulfed in bright flames, and from then until the next morning, about twenty houses, among which were a number of the most beautiful private residences of Springfield, had turned into ash. Perhaps it is true that, as the saying goes, an order was issued from above about which houses would fall prey to destruction. Certainly it had to seem incomprehensible to the sober judgment why the property of the enemy was destroyed once it was in one's hands and one had confidence to claim it. How many poor Union families who had fled to within the lines of our army would have been happy to find shelter in these houses? But it showed that the longer the Civil War lasted, the rougher and more ruthless the conduct of war became. During the first two times we occupied Springfield, not a single house had been destroyed, and now, within the first twelve hours, right in front of the guard and the main general, one house after the other fell. Was that coincidence?

And how about all the furnishings in these beautiful homes—the expensive furniture, the beautiful carpets, and the expensive pianos? These had either been brought to safety by the owners, or they burnt along with the house. One should believe me: The Southerners were quite unjust when they claimed again and again, after taking New Orleans, that the Northern officers had a special weakness for silver spoons. The ladies of the North would also desire pianos, and no one likes to see pianos burn. There was, for instance, in our army corps a colonel (he was supposed to have been a police officer in

Germany), who had sent home furniture instead of laurels during his campaigns in Missouri to decorate his home most luxuriously and fittingly from top to bottom. When he was transferred later to a state situated much further south and his wife came to visit, he gave the friendly advice to a local, wealthy family to leave their home immediately since it was in grave danger of being attacked at any moment. The attack did not occur, but the esteemed couple moved into the beautiful residence, enjoyed themselves there, and before moving back out, they had everything portable packed in large containers and sent to the far North. But even that was not enough. Even plants—the most beautiful in the garden—were dug out and had to come along, and what did not meet with the taste of the colonel, such as books, he offered to his comrades.

"We don't need this for ourselves; we have enough," the dedicated colonel said, "But we have a little girl, and she will have a wedding soon, and this will make a nice dowry for her." This colonel was renowned for being diligent, if a bit strict, and he was certain to become general soon. Although, this furniture export accounted only for a small item on his registry of sins.

VIII.
A Chivalrous Enemy.
A Mysterious Maneuver. War Atrocities.

On a hill outside of Springfield, we encountered a large number of barracks that might have been used by approximately one division of the enemy army. These barracks had been offered to us as quarters, and we were eager to find out what kind of winter abodes our enemies had prepared for themselves. Our barracks were long buildings; half were log-houses and half were frame houses, and they were so spacious that more than half a battalion could be housed. Three wide beds bunked on top of each other. The lack of light and ventilation gave them a great similarity to the 'tween-deck of an emigrant ship, and it provided a fertile ground for vermin and illnesses. In comparison, the enemy barracks were small and low log-houses, sided and patched up with clay and well secured against wind and cold. They were either longer buildings divided inside by walls into completely separated rooms, or they were freely standing small houses. All of them were characterized by well-built brick fireplaces and a somewhat cozy interior. No wonder our boys saw them with big eyes and had reason to reflect, for a soldier must reflect, and even more so the more comfort he enjoys.

In the adjacent buildings of a former farmhouse—which was designated by an inscription as the quarters of the commissioner—we found, to our great joy, still some supplies of flour, fresh ham, and dried apple slices. It was just enough for this and the next day's food supply for us. That means adding insult to injury:[30] we burn down the secessionist houses, or they give us shelter and food. Truly, this Price guy must have been a humane, charming man, or he must have left in a great hurry. Without his provisions, we would have had to spend the rest of the day and night, again, without food under the open sky at freezing temperatures, which became worse from hour to hour. Our few wagons reached us on this day and brought us knapsacks, but they had to turn around to fetch those goods that were unloaded or thrown

Figure 19. General Sterling Price. *Harper's Weekly*, October 12, 1861.

---

[30] The literal translation of this statement is "gathering gleaming coals on top of the enemy's head."

aside on the way—those which the delivery men, under the command of a caring[31] quartermaster, had smashed or had preferred to let lay at the side of the road.

[I still have to mention another legacy of the enemy: A few severely ill had been left behind in one of the barracks under the care of one doctor. They, too, did not wear a trace of a uniform, and they enjoyed no comfort. The doctor, a younger gentleman, almost childishly—as open and innocent in his appearance as in his speech, and proud not to have abandoned the ill—told us that his army had departed last night and that it numbered ten thousand to twelve thousand men. It consisted entirely of Missourians with the exception of the artillery, their main force. He also told us that Price would not confront the Union army in this region. He had not intended to do so even in the fall of last year, but he intended to retreat as far as the territory of Arkansas for reinforcement by Southern troops, which were promised to him in significant numbers. When asked whether he received pay—a very significant aspect!—he responded that doctors were not paid at all. Besides, he only had little hope that the revolution would succeed, and he even regretted to have joined that cause. He told all this to one of our doctors with whom he had attended one of the medical colleges in St. Louis, and whom he had met for the first time after several years.]

---

[31] "Caring" is used sarcastically here.

Wilson's Creek, February 14, 1862

One can imagine our joy was not great when we had to leave our warm barracks the next morning in order to chase after the enemy while our wagons with tents and provisions had not yet reached us[, and we had to leave our knapsacks behind for accelerating the march.] A frosty chill and a sharp wind blew in our faces, the ground was covered with ice, and our beards were ornate with icicles. We took comfort, however, in hearing that the enemy had taken up a firm position at Wilson's Creek and that we would encounter him there to settle the old score. A few also cheered themselves up in this bad frost by the thought that the enemy is twice as sensitive and disadvantaged in this cold because he is not used to it. They had been deceived twice: The enemy consisted almost exclusively of Missourians who were not any less used to this climate than we were, and the enemy was not even thinking about going into battle.

We had gone about two miles when we found the First Division assembled in battle formation on a wide field. Our corps, too, had been ordered to take up position as reserve. Generals and aides rushed around, and everyone looked eager for battling the enemy. There, in front of us on a hill, we became aware of a long, dark row that seemed positioned before a line of trees. Our grand staff officers reached for their binoculars and discovered that it was nothing but fence rails.

After a while, the rows of the division positioned in front of us stirred agitatedly. [We saw convoys hurry around, but we were unable to discern an orderly battle maneuver. Soon, our soldiers put together their guns in pyramids and started, according to the example ahead of us, to dance around and to box and fight each other.] The cold drove the lads first to dance around and box each other and, then, to attack an existing fence nearby in order to start a new fire. A captain, who might have become impatient by this delay of several hours in such cold, turned to a higher ranking officer with the question of why it was we did not advance. He received the answer: "Price is not yet ready; we have to wait until he has also put his battle line into formation." This declaration might be less useful to explain our maneuver, but rather to characterize some officers in our volunteer army. These words were spoken in full earnest, and with the same seriousness, the captain had passed them along to our company.

Little York,[32] February 14, 1862

According to the position of the sun (all our watches had stopped), it was close to noon when the battle line dissolved again and the train started to move as usual. A path of about ten miles brought us to Little York, a little town that consisted of not more than two short rows of houses on both sides of the street. [How much of it still stands today, I cannot say with certainty.] When we arrived, the outermost house stood in flames and—as it became a legendary anecdote—when the last part of our train passed through, only smoking ruins were left standing.

Here, two companies of our unrelenting German cavalry had chased off the end of the enemy's train the evening before. They had taken away a substantial number of wagons and brought them back to Springfield. We had found, as the victims of the skirmish, the corpses of a few secessionists in the woods bordering the road[,and in a neighboring house, a wounded soldier—a boy of not eighteen years of age, who was holding up pretty well even though a bullet had entered his right chest, next to the sternum, and exited next to the spine.] These were

---

[32] Little York was a town near present-day Brookline, Missouri.

the corpses of young boys and of old men who paid with their lives for trying to drive the wagons of the enemy army to bring supplies to their relatives and friends. One of our officers recognized a wealthy old farmer and judge from the Kansas border, and he told how one day during bloody skirmishes between the border regions of Missouri and Kansas at the beginning of the Civil War, this old man had returned to his home and seen how Kansas people had attacked his house, hanged his son, and abused his wife who was left in a delirious state. And now, even the head of the family had fallen prey to the curse of slavery.

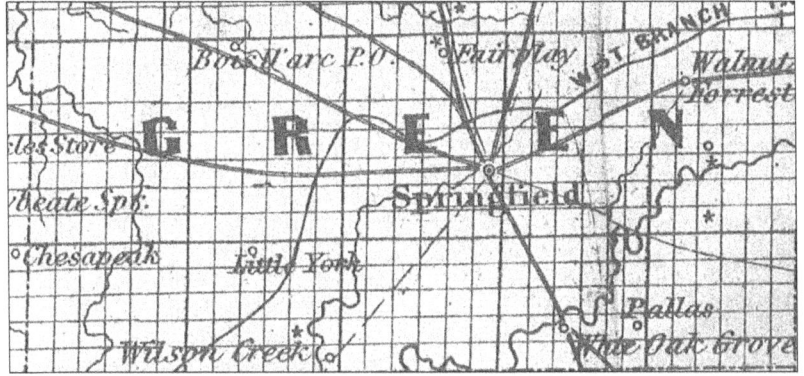

Figure 20. Map of Little York. *Colton's Sectional Map of Missouri*, 1869.

A few miles outside Little York on a wide, rocky prairie, we stopped, and the various troop units were assigned their quarters for the coming night. We never had a camp that was less inviting. A dilapidated log-house had been elevated as main quarters, in which the general with his staff resided. Closely next to it, in a sparsely wooded area—if it was deserving of such a description—our troops looked for protection from the harsh winds. The cold, which had been alleviated slightly by the sun at noon, had again reached its former iciness. Only one wagon with a few tents had gotten hold of us. Firewood was sparse, and groceries consisted mainly of a few sheep, a calf, and geese that had crossed our path in Little York and that we had dragged on as prisoners of war.

[I was among the most fortunate. In order not to expose our limbs too much to frost and rheumatism—which had become epidemic—and for lack of tents and blankets, I looked together with other officers for shelter in a little frame house 1½ miles away from the regiment and close to our outposts. The house and the barn stood empty; an old, maggot-infested bed was the only thing that the owner left behind. Our first business was to break it to pieces and to make a big fire in the fireplace. The second was to nail up the windows of broken glass with boards in order to protect ourselves from the biting draft. Then, our guys dispersed in all directions to find whatever might prove useful under such circumstances. Feed for our horses and straw for our beds were the first and most necessary items they brought in. A bag of wheat flour and a pot full of lard, which was found in the neighboring shack, were most welcome. Water, however, which had to be carried from two miles away, looked more like coffee dregs. It was, after closer inspection, nothing but dirt in fluid form.

In spite of that, we felt more and more comfortable sitting on wooden blocks around the bright, warm fire, and as night approached, we had been so plentifully served that we missed nothing for our bliss, least of all a healthy appetite for dinner. A coffee kettle, a skillet, a bag full of coffee, and another with sugar were always brought along by our guys, and behind us, a few fat geese—which had been captured on the way—screamed and rolled around on the floor with their feet tied. So we proceeded to light our pipes and began to improvise a civilized meal with the means present. One guy beheaded the prisoners, two scraped them—since there was neither enough light nor patience to pluck them—and a fourth guy gutted them, drained the goose fat, and mixed—together with the flour and the so-called water—the dough to a kind of pancake. A fifth man finally poured a good amount of coffee beans—roasted, as delivered by our government—into a dirty knapsack, the cleanest item that could be found on us, and beat the knapsack with a piece of wood until the coffee was "ground." Satisfied and exhausted, we lay down on the straw (it was late) to fall quickly into a deep slumber and—with the extinguished fire and the arrival of the severe morning frost—to freeze until we were stiff.]³³

IX.
Our Lives' Elixir. Long Marches and Little Sleep. Future Hospitals and Destruction by Fire.

On the morning after the freezing night, a few of our wagons appeared in time for our departure. They brought the knapsacks and enough food to hand a hot cup of coffee and a biscuit to every soldier. This was the only nourishment available before the evening, and for some, the only nourishment since the morning before. Biscuit or hard bread replaces, in the American army, the commissioned bread, and it has the advantages of tasting better and not spoiling as quickly. It was of good quality; made of white ship's rusk, the square-shaped bars were often hard as stone and

Figure 21. Hard tack.
Photo courtesy of Dennis Hood.

---

³³ This is the point where the first narrative ends.

made of good wheat flour that had been supplied in sufficient quantities until this point.

The most valuable thing the American soldier received, however, was the coffee, either green or roasted, always in sufficient quantity, and of a good kind. One time we received, as an experimental replacement, a thick syrup that contained ingredients such as concentrated coffee, milk, and sugar, which, however, did not pay off. The coffee is a replacement for those alcoholic drinks that in the army and the navy of the United States is not delivered and is even prohibited—for good reason! For one thing, it is paramount not to have people get used to brandy,[34] which is even more paramount since the American and the inlander[35] know no measure in drinking, and since in the Regular army, alcohol addiction is like cancer under which officers and soldiers suffer. On the other hand, we convinced ourselves that the effect of coffee lasts longer and is more invigorating and warming than brandy. With a cup of coffee in the body and a few biscuits in the bread bag, packed with a knapsack, a woolen blanket, a field canister, an ax, and a kettle, a soldier marches the whole day through frost and rain and crosses creeks and rivers, the water of which often reaches his chest. He generally indulges in no long stop until arriving at the night camp in the evening, and once he dries himself at the fire and warms himself with a cup of coffee, he feels newly invigorated and holds watch without hesitation and without letting himself indulge with comfort in the quiet enjoyment of a pipe of tobacco. Often, I had the impression that I never felt better after a meal than at those that resembled noon and evening meals simultaneously, made of coffee, biscuit, and a piece of fried ham or bacon.

---

[34] It is possible the author is indicating whiskey when referring to brandy in America.

[35] The author is probably referring to American Indians.

This day, the coffee worked its wonders as well. It strengthened us for the longest daily march that we had covered in this campaign. We marched without interruption until four o'clock in the afternoon. The weather favored us; the sun shone the whole day, and for a few days, we again had the most beautiful spring weather. This is how we experienced winter in the entire South, from the Missouri River all the way down to the Gulf of Mexico. First, there were three to eight days of mild warmth, then, thunderstorms and rain, and with that, the arrival of freezing cold, which lasted two to three days.

How cheerfully we greeted the arrival of our wagons on this evening! How voraciously we attacked their supplies to prepare a solid meal and to thoroughly quench our appetite! Then came the order not to erect tents, but to cook, fill our bread sacks for the next day, and lie down and be ready for departure right after midnight. It was two o'clock when we reported the next morning, but it took an entire hour until the train started moving. Daily, at every departure, the same scene repeated itself: We had to untangle the path in front of us, blocked by a knot of wagons, from unorganized regiments, or we repeatedly had to stop in order to let cavalry and artillery pass by. Nothing tired the troops more than such a delay, and such delays did not only happen during departure, but also often during the march. Here, again was revealed—as it was in anything else—the lack of organization, exercise, and discipline within the American army. The troops became exhausted and suffered often from being deprived of necessities, and their movement was clumsy and slow. No wonder Price with his light-footed Missourians escaped us. At first, they had a lead of about six to eight hours. To this day, our advance guard, consisting of cavalry and mounted artillery, had not managed to stop even the rear guard of the enemy.

A second mistake of our marches was that we made stops that were regular and long. With the exception of those involuntary, exhausting delays, we marched from morning to early in the evening from one respite to the other. For that day, this was beneficial because all of us suffered from such sleep deprivation that whoever sat down for a moment fell asleep immediately and could be awakened only with great effort. Half asleep, the soldiers marched. My horse lowered its head and plodded with closed eyes between the foot soldiers, and my own head also bowed down, being jerked up every ten minutes whenever my bent-over head was threatening me to lose my balance. In a forest that extended for a distance along the road, our sleeping warriors lay everywhere, often in groups underneath a protruding rock like groundhogs in their cave, immersed in such a deep sleep that the greatest commotion on the road would not be able to wake them up.

In the American army, it is customary to put in a day of rest after three days marching. On our present pursuit march, this custom was not observed; however, to provide at least half a day of rest, we camped at two o'clock already. Here, our train caught up with us as well, and for the first time in five days, we had the opportunity to sleep in tents again.

Cassville, Ceatsville, February 16, 1862

This camp was located at the onset of a pleasant, more densely populated and well-cultivated landscape. There, a wide valley with meadows stretched out in front of us bordered by wooded hilltops and traversed by a river, which activated several mills, and a road, at which several small (and one large) farms and two little towns were located. The first little town, named Cassville, consisted of several streets and many shops and other stores, and it had at its center a large, stone courthouse. The second town, about one mile away from Cassville, consisted of little more than one row of modest wood houses and a large, stately, and also wooden, house surrounded by farm buildings. The dwelling is named after Mr. Ceats, the owner, according to custom in the West that towns and dwellings are named after their oldest and wealthiest inhabitant.

Now, most of the houses in both of these towns stood empty. Three weeks later, they all were densely populated by the injured and wounded of our army. In the church and the little wooden houses of Ceatsville[36] lay our wounded Germans, put on straw without any comfort, but nevertheless, enjoying a

---

[36] The author includes a footnote on the side of the page explaining the town is also spelled "Keatsville."

comparatively good state of health. The wounded Americans, and also many of their ill, were taken to Cassville. They filled the rooms of the courthouse and other larger buildings. Their number was much more considerable and their care much better, since the hospital supplies and other goods arriving directly from St. Louis got into their hands first. On the other hand, amassing in larger locations and putting together wounded and typhoid patients had the consequence of typhoid spreading frightfully, and one year later, long after the hospital had been closed and the little town had been turned to ash by a second Union army, a large cemetery marked the place where Cassville had stood and where the wounded of Pea Ridge had found asylum.

X.
Plundering Knights. At the Border of Arkansas.
A Future and Fresh Battlefield.

Our march led through a valley of meadows and both towns described above. An incident unfolded before our eyes, which is mentioned because it is a reminder of a black spot in our soldiers' lives: namely, the stealing of horses committed by commoners and officers, and which neither friend nor enemy had been spared, not even regarding horses that were privately owned by officers. This afternoon, an older farmer came riding to our convoy on a mediocre horse. He rode down the embankment of the road and made as wide a detour as the terrain would allow. One officer spotted him, rode toward him, called for some soldiers, and forced the surprised rider to dismount by claiming that an old, blurred branding, to which the letter "O" had been prefixed, would prove that this animal belonged to the Rebel army. The farmer insisted that the horse had been in his possession forever and that the branding could impossibly have been a "CS"—the insignia of the Confederate States. But in vain! The boy of the officer mounted into the saddle and rode off with the horse, and the officer bragged and laughed about how he now would have one additional horse. The farmer, however, ran meanwhile along the convoy to its lead and pleaded with a few officers.

But as he lamented his sorrow, someone close by sensed a revolver in his pocket: "Hulloh, fellow! You are carrying weapons with you. Get them out!"And for better or worse, even the revolver had to be handed over.

"And now see that you disappear, Rebel! Quickly! Away with you, or ..."

The cheated had no other choice but to expediently disappear in the bushes. But a farmer will not relinquish a trade so easily, not even in America. Such a farmer was used to drumming up the entire neighborhood against horse thieving and to hanging the captured from a tree with his own hands. And now he should accept to having his horse stolen from right between his legs? No. In the evening at our camp, suddenly, the old farmer turned to the general with his laments and received his horse back.

Pea Ridge, February 19, 1862

A few miles beyond the last little town, we climbed down a deep gorge that, at first narrow and then wider and wider, expanded for several miles in between the high mountain ranges. At the steep embankment of the rough road, and often covering half of it, lay massive tree trunks. Apparently, the enemy had blocked the path with those to delay our advance for several hours, and our advance guard had only partially moved them to the side. Here was the border between Missouri and Arkansas. When we crested the border, the banging of heavy artillery resonated from the mountains. Shot after shot rolled like distant thunder through the gorges and mountains. After more than half an hour, it became quiet again—dusk was setting in—and we camped for the first time on the territory of Arkansas. The following morning, our way led us to the other end of the valley and up a steep hill. From here, a wide plateau expanded on both sides of the road—mostly open, cultivated land and, intermittently, a short stretch of woods.

First, we encountered to the right of the road a large, wooden tavern named Elkhorn Tavern; and behind it, along the road, a narrow, lighter forest; and to the right of that, a sudden pasture grown with high trees and covered with a few gigantic rocks that designated the highest spot of this landscape and was called Pea Ridge. The battle that ensued fourteen days later in this area and which was decided at this spot, we named after the tavern, while the Southerners named it Pea Ridge.

Figure 22. Battle of Pea Ridge. *Harper's Weekly*, March 29, 1862.

Sugar Creek, Bentonville, February 19, 1862

Our country road led us for a long stretch over the plateau. Then, it went down a steep, wooded decline into a deep valley, which—similar to the one we had just traversed—was about six to eight miles long and cut through the plateau from east to west. In the midst of this valley, a river meandered—its name, Sugar Creek—at which the road forks. One arm leads through the length of the valley with the other crossing upwards to a lower hill. At this spot, our advance guard had encountered the rear guard of the enemy, and a small skirmish ensued, from which, apparently, the enemy escaped advantageously. At least, they left no dead or wounded on our hands. On and next to the road, we found a number of dead horses, and in a nearby house lay our dead—eleven in number—stretched out. I recognized among them no old acquaintance, but easily, from the expression of the dead, the nationality to which each of them belonged: here, with the small, narrow face, the long neck, the sharply contoured nose, and the thin lips, the American; there, the round, full face of the German; and next, the red, curly hair of the Irish, with a pronounced jaw, the broad cheekbones, and the snub nose. Our less wounded were quartered at a nearby log-house whose inhabitants had to share their modest accommodations with them. Out of gratitude, this house was burnt down fourteen days later, "for strategic reasons," they said.

On the meadows along Sugar Creek, we opened our quarters and rested the following day, which was more than welcome because rain, joined by a frost, followed. During this rest, an accident occurred that is not rare considering the carelessness of our soldiers. Two of our men started a fire close to a few munitions crates and sat down on them while smoking and talking in order to warm themselves at the fire. Suddenly, a bang followed, and our warriors flew in the air and into a near ditch. Without receiving much damage, however, with burnt clothes and their faces and hands black as Negroes, they were picked up by their comrades and brought to the other wounded in that log-house, from where they returned a few weeks later hardened and marked by many little blue dots.

XI.
Notorious Enemy. Bands of Thieves.
Land and People of Arkansas.

While the infantry reposed thus at Sugar Creek, our cavalry under General Asboth combed through the territory in front of us and took possession, first, of the little town of Bentonville, the main seat of the northwestern county of Arkansas. Here had been the main quarters of Southern General McCulloch, the same who, together with Price, had beaten the Union army under General Lyon last summer at Wilson's Creek. Ben McCulloch was a feared man— an almost mythical figure. He was one of those trappers or

Figure 23. General Ben McCulloch. *Harper's Weekly*, September 7, 1861.

border dwellers of Texas whose life consisted of a series of adventures and fights with Indians and Mexicans, and he enjoyed the reputation of being the most daring and skillful leader of trappers. With his name and the troops from Texas and Arkansas led by him, the Southern newspapers threatened with menacing pictures about fiends and giants. In old novels, the Texans and Arkansans enjoyed the reputation of being the most dangerous border fiends, and they were never imagined any different than with a Bowie knife, a bottle of Schnaps, and a revolver in every pocket of their tattered clothing.

A TEXAN RANGER.

WE publish above a sketch, by one of our most reliable artists, of a TEXAN RANGER. A gentleman, just from Richmond, gave the following account of these redoubtable warriors :

Ben McCullogh's Texan Rangers are described as a desperate set of fellows. They number one thousand half savages, each of whom is mounted upon a mustang horse. Each is armed with a pair of Colt's navy revolvers, a rifle, a tomahawk, a Texan bowie-knife, and a lasso. They are described as being very dexterous in the use of the latter. These men are to be pitted against Wilson's Zouaves and McMullin's Rangers.

Figure 24. A Texas Ranger. *Harper's Weekly*, July 6, 1861.

By themselves, such people are not used to forming independent corps of troops, but they were integrated into a larger army. Thus, their boisterousness was quickly broken, and military order and uniformity erased their individuality. That happened to the feared troops of McCulloch. He himself enjoyed great popularity among his troops and much respect from us because he treated his prisoners very well. The Texan infantry gained the reputation of great bravery in distant Virginia under their General Hood, as well as in the West, namely where the attempted storming of Corinth earned them the admiration of the victorious army under General Rosecrans, as well as of the entire North. The Texan horsemen, called Texas Rangers—characterized by their small, extremely enduring horses, Texan Ponies—found, from the beginning, comrades in the Southern cavalry who equaled their courage and daringness.

We generally found the prejudice of the troops and inhabitants of Arkansas completely unjustified; however, around that time, a certain group of people appeared who completely lived up to the stereotypical reputation. Since then, they have become the terror of northern Arkansas—the border region toward Missouri that is wooded, partly mountainous, and partly swamp. Namely, they were formally organized bands of thieves and murderous arsonists consisting of old desperados and horse thieves from here up to Kansas, known as Jayhawkers. They belonged to no party. With great neutrality, they pillaged Union men and Southern sympathizers equally. Their politics were to steal horses and mules and, on occasion, to also rob and pillage other items. Wherever there were no Northern or Southern troops close by, they appeared and took from the poor people whatever they had left in their possession. Even across the Mississippi in western Tennessee such bands wreaked havoc. There, they consisted mostly of deserters of the Southern army and had been falsely labeled guerillas. Close by, outside of Memphis and its northern advance guards, they wreaked havoc, attacked and robbed everyone they could lay hands on, burnt down houses, shot or hanged their inhabitants, and beat or whipped Negroes literally to death. In short, they committed atrocities fueled by their addiction to violence, gruesomeness, and personal vengeance. After the war was over, when the Southern soldiers returned home and the Northern garrisons stayed around the country, the Jayhawkers disappeared at once. Some of them felt somewhat constricted when encountering those who returned home, or they felt their throats severely tied up, and that occasioned everyone who still had time to get a change of air in the far away territories or in the wide countryside of Texas!

Our march the next day led us through the entire length of the meadow valley and, then, to the gradually elevated rolling landscape where magnificent forests; large, well-cultivated fields and pastures; several towns; and large, stately farms offered a surprisingly friendly impression. They indicated that we were not any longer in Missouri, but in a completely different part of the country. Sixteen to eighteen miles from our last camp and about three miles southeast of the little town of Bentonville, we put up our tents on a lower, flat hill situated under fruit trees, and we enjoyed with uninterrupted spring weather a rest of eight days after our campaign had lasted only three weeks.

At this time—and even more so two months later when we entered the territory of Arkansas for the second time far more to the east—we were most pleasantly surprised by the difference regarding country and people compared to southern Missouri. Yes, our farmer boys from Illinois opened their eyes wide; this was certainly a different nature than that of their fertile, yet, so unspeakably boring prairies. Where else do they have, as they generally do on the other side of the Mississippi, such forests and such a wealth of springs, creeks, and rivers with the clearest water, and full of fish! We shouted and cheered and believed we were back home[37] when we rode through these majestic forests with their gigantic, proud trunks and the lush foliage. And how astonished we were as we suddenly entered a wide clearing and before us lay a large farm—an incredible, fenced-in square of well-cultivated fields, fruit gardens, and pastures, including dwellings and farm buildings. This is a characteristic of Arkansas: Individual farms or complexes of smaller ones are located within forests, and it is always a most pleasant sight for us to look at these wide, light-green fields encircled by high forest lines and covered by a blue sky. The splendor of color must be even more beautiful in the fall, when the tree foliage would cover the fields like snow.

The products grown here—which are used mostly for domestic purposes—are wheat and corn, which had almost entirely replaced cotton production since the outbreak of the war. Also locally grown are tobacco, potatoes—especially the so-called sweet potatoes—and a heavy amount of fruit, such as apples and peaches, and in the vicinity of Little Rock, also white American wine, which is produced by German farmers from the Catawba grape and has much similarity with the Mosel wine.[38] There are no large cotton plantations here; those are located more to the south in swamp regions along the great rivers. Here, in the northern part of Arkansas, the so-called slave-owning aristocracy did not reside, neither in the forest farms nor in the wide open stretches of land that were all agriculturally cultivated around Bentonville. Residing here were, more or less, wealthy farmers who grew everything they needed for themselves. These people, just as the settlers of southern Missouri, were almost all immigrants, mostly from Kentucky, and they were the most enlightened and adroit. They also originated from the poor mountainous regions of the

---

[37] The author is likely referring to Germany.
[38] *Moselwein* refers to a traditional wine region in Germany.

South, such as eastern Tennessee, North Carolina, and northern Georgia.

We saw only a few colored people; with the exception of aging, weak house slaves and children, they all had been driven south, together with cattle and horses. The white male population, at least all the young men, was gone from the homes. Where? That was an easy guess. Women and children remained mostly at home in order to protect their possessions by their presence. Yes, in the eastern part of northern Arkansas, into which we marched later, a larger number of young men did stay home, many of which had fled from Southern conscription officers, and now hundreds of them came to our main quarters in order to take an oath of allegiance toward the United States and to receive in return a confirming document. These would safeguard them from confiscations and acquisitions (but it still happened that the army was in need of supplies), and then, they received a money order from the government for all the goods they supplied, which could be retrieved from a quartermaster or a government official, or which could be sold just like a check.

Almost daily I roamed the environment, either alone or accompanied by a comrade, and dismounted in front of one of the other beautiful farm houses, which reminded me of Illinois by their pleasant appearance. It was my intent to get to know land and people and also, in part, to trade for food, such as eggs, dried fruit, and sweet potatoes. Usually, by my friendly address and the showing of silver coins—many still had little trust in United States paper money—I succeeded in overcoming shyness and suspicion of the house inhabitants. But if their antagonistic spirit made them insist that they had nothing, then I resorted to my last means, which never failed to impress the women: I got from one of the two saddlebags a little bag of coffee, the favorite beverage of all women, which had become a rarity since the beginning of the war and was to be had only with much money. The fondling of that bag and the pleasant aroma of coffee beans, of which they had been deprived for so long, when rolled over the table, always worked like a divining rod. Within half an hour the table was adorned with all that kitchen and pantry had to offer, and fortune was once again smiling at me with a white, clean tablecloth and shiny dishes, on which there were foods that, for the soldiers, resembled a feast, but was common for the farmer: fresh milk, still scalding little rolls, a piece of fried chicken, scrambled eggs, vegetables, and what was never amiss from the American farmer's table—freshly baked cornbread and, as supplement, butter and molasses (syrup made from sugarcane).

The women also became more talkative when, after the meal, they offered chairs next to themselves and began to smoke their pipes. Smoking tobacco, which is seen only rarely with women in the North and, then only with Irish women, is a much more common custom among women in the country in the South, especially among the older, wealthier ones. This, however, is not the case with female planters. The tobacco is self grown; the pipe consists of a piece of reed and a clay head or, when unavailable, hollowed corn cobs. These women in northern Arkansas belonged to the best I came to know in America. They belonged to the splendid kind of American farmers' wives who are the opposite of those beguiling, lazy, demanding, affected, and weak ladies of the cities or towns in the North and the South, and they are the opposite of the lazy, tremendously uneducated, quite unhappy women of the poor population within the cotton states. The women here are healthy, strong, modest, and diligent like our German farmers' wives, but they are more fluent in conversation and social interaction and masters in domestic duties. They stand out with their love for order and cleanliness, which is unsurpassable. Here in Arkansas, as is otherwise the case in the South, the female chores include working at the loom (Northern farmers' wives do not know of that). In every somewhat well-situated house, I saw a loom at which women weaved cloth from self-grown cotton. They colored it with oak bark and, with their own hands, manufactured clothing for their men, children, and slaves—rugged red and yellow clothing, which had been predominantly worn by the male population of the South before the war, and exclusively worn during the war.

XII.
Soldier's Household. The Hostage of War.
A Poisoning and Its Consequences.

We were positioned in this beautiful Arkansas under our fruit trees and were leisurely. The land, however, paid the rent. Our own supplies were exhausted; fresh shipments were sparse since Texas Rangers had meddled in our region and had partly destroyed and partly robbed one of our large provisions convoys. This made it necessary for us to send out small expeditions with empty wagons to look for supplies that were sometimes found hidden in large ditches or behind haystacks. They frequently returned with pigs, bacon, wheat, and corn flour, or feed for our animals. Sometimes, they also brought sweet potatoes and, occasionally, full wagon loads of the most beautiful apples. Then, we butchered mercilessly, fried, and baked. When walking through the camp, one encountered, literally, mounds of loaves that were made from flour and pigs' lard, baked with or without apples, as a replacement for bread and biscuits. Coffee was missing; instead of it, almost everyone drank the red tea made of sassafras wood. This tea enjoys the reputation in medicine of purifying blood, and even more so among the people here. Now, since coffee and tea had vanished from the country, sassafras tea became the widely popular beverage in Arkansas. Even our soldiers and officers eagerly gathered the shrubbery that grew plentifully in these woods, and they amused themselves with combining the pleasant with the necessary—turning a chore into a spring therapy.

While our infantry was thus engaged in domestic duties and healthcare and used the land in a manner that was considered permissible in war, our horsemen were tirelessly absorbed in reconnaissance and mercilessly held the unfortunate area a hostage of war. The pretty little town of Bentonville was their first victim. When our cavalry took possession of it and left it immediately afterward, one soldier was supposed to be left behind; supposedly, his corpse was found during the second arrival of our troops. Neither I nor any of my friends were able to find out how much truth was contained in this dark and contradictory rumor. To no avail, Bentonville had to pay for that. At our arrival, we found its main streets burnt down, and we could recognize from the smoking ruins that many important shops, stores, taverns, and churches had stood there.

Next, it was the turn of other towns [three miles east of our camp]. In the first, the Southern troops had left behind a small hospital. Some of our cavalry officers entered it and demanded brandy. When told there wasn't any, they examined the bottles of medicine, thought they found in one of them a magenbitter,[39] and drank it with gusto. Apparently, this medicinal beverage was made of a local poisonous plant, for within only a brief time, all who had tasted it suffered from the most acute symptoms of poisoning. One captain[40] passed away, and two other officers narrowly avoided the same fate. Under different circumstances, one would have seen a well-deserved punishment for the brutality and drinking addictions of these officers. In war, however, there is no sober and just sentence—only passion and excitement. This incident is a crass example of how war produces false rumors, how they become widely dispersed and are generally believed, and how they generate hate and cruelty. In the entire North, and even in Europe, the news-

---

[39] This is an alcoholic beverage that is supposed to cure stomach ailments. It is also known today by the brand Jägermeister.
[40] Captain Louis Dulfer

papers reported how officers of the Union army had been killed by food poisoning in Arkansas, and they used the opportunity to speak about the hair-raising barbarism of the Southern people. On the other hand, nothing was said of the barbarism of those who had, in blind wrath, laid that town, as well as another neighboring town, into ashes.

When, a few days later, a junior officer of that cavalry reported that incident in my presence, he asked whether we could remember how, the day of our entry into Springfield, a number of wagons of the enemy train had been taken by us close to the little town of York, and a few of their drivers were massacred. When we affirmed that we did remember, he continued: "I am an old soldier and not exactly soft of heart, but my blood stopped flowing in my veins when the commanding officer gave the order to slay the defenseless drivers—old men and boys—and when he himself shot down the first one. This officer was the same captain who died of the poison. By God! Wasn't that a retaliation?"

And all this was only the beginning of the misery that engulfed this region! For a long, long time the hurricane of the Civil War waged here; again and again, hordes of one party, and then of the other, stormed over this territory, and the longer the war lasted, the more merciless and bitter it became. Both armies, which confronted each other at this spot, were still to be called human and well-disciplined in comparison to those coming after them and offering each other battle in this region. Truly, this countryside must have resembled an image of devastation at the end of the war similar to the lower regions of Louisiana when the swollen waters of the Mississippi had breached its levies and had turned the bountiful plantations into marshes and swamps!

Commentary of the Transcriber
Klaus Trobisch, 80 Years Old
Frankfurt, Germany

I find the text enormously interesting, and I am glad to get to read the material in this form (original, handwritten German script). I always had thought of the American Civil War as something of a leisurely stroll, but now I continue to learn.

Many greetings, Klaus.

Poem Composed in Honor of the Siblings Who Returned from America on May 10, 1870

Zum Empfang der l. Geschwister,
Alexander und Julie aus Amerika,
den 10. Mai 1870.

Willkommen aus fernen Landen
Ihr theuern Geschwister allhier.
Ob fern nach dem Leibe, verbanden,
uns Liebe und Treu für und für..

Willkommen von weiter Reise,
da Gott Euch so freundlich geführt,
zurück zum heimischen Kreise.
Dank ihm von Herzen gebührt.

Willkommen mit Freudenthränen,
wie schlägt uns so fröhlich das Herz,
nach Euch ging unser Sehnen,
das Eure heimathwärts.

Nun seid ihr wirklich gekommen.
Es ist wie ein schöner Traum.
Wir haben euch wieder gewonnen,
wir sehen's und glauben es kaum.

Ihr habt es nun reichlich erfahren,
bald von Herzen erfreut, bald
betrübt.

Gott leitet treu uns aus Gefahren
zum Besten dem, der ihn liebt.

A welcome to the first Siblings,
Alexander and Julie from America
May 10, 1870

Welcome from lands afar
you valuable siblings here.
Whether distant in person,
love and faith connected us forever.

Welcome from expansive travels,
from where God has led so kindly,
back to the circles of home.
Thanks to Him from our hearts.

Welcome with tears of joy,
how happy beat our hearts,
after you our longing went out
which has brought you homeward.

Now you have really arrived.
It is like a beautiful dream.
We have won you back again,
we see it, yet, hardly believe it.

You have it now plentifully
experienced, joyful in heart at times,
at others saddened.

God leads us faithfully out of
dangers toward the best who loves

Willkommen, seid herzlich willkommen, umschlungen mit alter Lieb.	Him. Welcome, you are heartily welcome, embraced by old love.
Gott schenke uns Tage der Wonnen, genug von dem, was uns so trieb.	God present us with days of joy enough of that which drove us.
Was bringt uns die Schwester für Gaben Entsprossen der neuen Welt, denn liebliche Blümchen sie haben zum Gruße von dort ausgewählt.	What gifts does our sister bring us emerging from the new world, they have lovely flowers as a greeting chosen from there.
Wir danken den Eltern, beiden, für diese Blümlein so fein, gewiss, wir wollen mit Freuden liebe Onkel und Tanten sein.	We thank the parents, both, for these flowers so fine, certainly we want to be with joy dear uncles and aunts to them.
Es falle der Großeltern Segen wie der Thau des Himmels auf sie, verlasse auf allen Wegen in Jugend und Alter sie nie.	The grandparents blessings may fall like dew from heaven unto them and never leave them on all paths in their youth and in their age.
Willkommen, willkommen sei allen, wir liebten, wir lieben euch noch, zu Ehren euch möge erschallen ein herzliches "Lebehoch!"	Welcome, welcome to you all, we love, we love you still, in honor of you may we all loudly pronounce a hearty "Cheers!"
J. R.	J.R.[41]

---

[41] This poem was added to the manuscript. Unfortunately, we cannot confirm that its contents refer to the author of the *Recollections*. If it does, the author's first name is Alexander, and the initial of his last name may be "R." His wife's first name, apparently, is Julie. According to the poem, they have at least two children, referred to as "flowers." Since the poem has been composed in honor of the siblings, the poem's author might have been Alexander's brother. Since the grandparents are mentioned, the purpose of Alexander and Julie's visit may have been to receive the grandparents' blessings for their children according to a German custom. It appears that the family is visiting Germany with the intention of returning back home to the United States. All this is speculative, and again, we encourage our readers to assist us in finding the identity of the author of the *Recollections*. We would be thrilled to acknowledge your participation in a second edition of this book.

Original German Manuscript

Tagebuch eines Missouri-Freiwilligen

An der Gasconade, Februar 2. 1862

Als Curtis das Commando über die bei Rolla, der äußersten Station der unvollendeten von St. Louis nach dem Südwesten Missouris gehenden Eisenbahn, im Winterquartier gelegenen Südwestarmee, übernahm, erließ er eine Generalordre an dieselben, worin er ihnen einen Feldzug durch „eine rauhe und öde Landschaft" ankündigte. Wir kannten diese Landschaft; sie brauchte nicht genannt zu werden; uns allen war sie noch in lebhafter Erinnerung von unserem letzten Rückzuge von Springfield her. Ich habe noch nie eine größere Thierquälerei gesehen als die, welche auf demgenannten Marsche, namentlich von Buffalo an bis zur Gasconade unseren Mauleseln widerfuhr; ich bin aber auch nie armseligeren und unwissenderen Menschen begegnet als in dieser einöden Gegend, die noch immer so aussieht, als ob nur Indianer und Kaninchen da hausten. Wir waren hier in Blockhäuser getreten (denn Frainhäuser sind hier eine Seltenheit, und Steinhäuser erinnere ich mich nicht gesehen zu haben), deren Bewohner, als wir ihnen für eine Mahlzeit, bestehend in Kornbrot, Molasses und Speck, eine Vergütung gaben, nicht einmal das dargereichte Silbergeld kannten.

Unsere Division war die letzte, welche Marschbefehl erhielt. 8 volle Tage wurde die Befolgung desselben verschoben, da uns die nöthigste Zahl von Wagen für Gepäck und Proviant fehlte, trotzdem alles irgendwie entbehrliche zurückgelassen und wir selber um ein Gutes zusammengeschmolzen waren, indem eine große Zahl Schwächlicher und Kranker theils aus dem Dienste entlassen, theils im Spital zu Rolla zurückgelassen wurde. Während dieser 8 Tage hatte aber auch der Himmel mit Regen, Schnee und Frost sein Möglischstes gethan, um uns von dem bevorstehenden Marsche das Schlimmste befürchten zu lassen.

Wirklich rechtfertige unser erster Tagemarsch diese Befürchtungen vollständig. Kaum 100 Schritte außerhalb des Bereiches der ehemaligen Lager, die wir durchzogen, blieb unser erster Wagen im Moraste stecken, und in nächster Nähe davon wurde unser ganzer Train zum Stehen gebracht durch einen Munitionswagen der Artillerie, den 10 Pferde vergeblich vom Flecke zu bringen suchten.

Rüstig zogen wir selber vorwärts durch den Schnee über das buschige Hügelland. Das Ziel unseres heutigen Marsches sollte die Stelle sein, wo die Little Piney in die Gasconade mündete. Noch 4 ½ Meilen davon entfernt machten wir Halt, um auf unseren Train zu warten. Doch derselbe erschien nicht, und so waren wir genöthigt auf dem Felde einer am Wege liegenden Farm zu bivouakieren. Auf

Ende der 1. Manuskriptseite

dem Schnee, einem äußerst frostigen Winde ausgesetzt, dabei ohne etwas Warmes im Leibe zu haben, verbrachten wir diese erste Nacht.

Einer kleinen Anzahl von uns war es vergönnt, in einer der 2 Blockhütten Obdach und Speise zu finden. Der Farmer war ein Unionsmann, ein echter Missourischer Unionsmann, wie wir sie zur Genüge konnten kennen lernen, äußerst kurz in seiner Rede, ohne jede Neigung, sich nach amerikanischem Brauche in ein Gespräch über Politik oder Krieg einlassen zu wollen, und offenbar sehr unzufrieden mit unsererm Besuche; ließ sich seinen Kaffee und Speck reichlich bezahlen, sogar für die Erlaubnis, auf dem Boden seiner Hütte schlafen zu dürfen, 25 Cents die Person, und war äußerst entrüstet, als seine unverschämte Rechnung für verbrannte Fenceziegel und einige geschossene Spahnferkel ganz bedeutend reducirt wurde. Auch sein Blockhaus war das Original der Behausung eines Missourischen Farmers, ein einfacher Raum mit zwei sich gegenüberstehenden Thüren ohne Schlößer und Riegel, dagegen mit einer Lücke im rohen Holz, durch welche die Hand hinausgestreckt wurde, um die fest anliegende, massive Thüre aufzureissen, natürlich auch ohne Fenster, dagegen voller Lücken und Löcher an Dach und Wänden, ein Muskitonetz, wie eines unserer Hauptleute es nannte der nicht Worte genug finden konnte, um seine Entrüstung auszudrücken über eine derartige Faulheit eines alten Ansiedlers mit 160 Acres guten Landes und ein paar erwachsenen Söhnen. Noch schlimmer sah übrigens das dahinter stehende kleinere Blockhaus drein, worin der eine Sohn mit einer hübschen jungen Frau und verschiedenen Sprößlingen hauste.

Auf dem Fußboden dieser Hütten lagen ohne weitere Unterlage als Decke als den Unterrock unsere meisten Officiere im Halbkreis ausgestreckt, die Füße dem Kamin zugekehrt, welcher, auf Steinen aufgethürmt, einem ans Haus hingebauten Festungsthurme voller Schießscharten glich und so umfänglich war, daß ein wahrer Scheiterhaufen von halben Baumstämmen darin loderte, dessen Hitze Einigen die Stiefel verbrannte, während ihr entfernter liegender Oberkörper empfindlich fror.

Diesen Morgen erschien unser Quartiermeister mit der angenehmen Nachricht, daß die Fuhrwerke noch immer nicht vom Flecke kämen. So mußten wir also nach der durchfrorenen Nacht auch noch eines erwärmenden Kaffees und überhaupt der Speise entsagen, einige Schweinchen abgerechnet, die von mehreren geschossen und gebraten wurden, und die paar Cräkers, welche der Eine und Andere glücklicherweise zu sich gesteckt hatte. Zur Erhöhung unserer angenehmen Lage erhob sich noch ein tüchtiges Schneegestöber, welches den ganzen Tag an bis in die Nacht hinein anhielt.

Endlich zwischen 2 und 3 Uhr trafen unsere Wagen ein; aber schon vorher war auch unser Genernal zurückgeritten gekommen, um sich nach der Ursache unseres Ausbleibens zu erkundigen und uns zu befehlen, sofort weiter zu marschieren. Es blieb uns aber eben Zeit, in aller Geschwindigkeit einen Kaffee zu sieden und dann die noch fehlenden 4 ½ Meilen zurückzulegen.

Es läßt sich denken, wie behaglich uns nach den durchlebten 2 Tagen gegenwärtig zu Muthe ist, da ich endlich in einem warmen Bette neben einer Tasse Thee mit Brandy auf meinem Feldbette

Ende der 2. Manuskriptseite

ausgestreckt liege und auf meinem Koffer diese Zeilen niederschreibe, ohne eine andere Sorge zu kennen als die, daß ich mit meinen Füßen den Boden berühren möchte, welcher, nach dem der Schnee unter der Ofenhitze geschmolzen, einen wahren Morast darstellt.

Big Piney, Febr. 4.

An e. kleinen Feuer stehend und die Füße erwärmend, benütze ich zur kurzen Skizzierung unseres gestrigen Marsche die Zeit, bis unsre Wagen und Artillerie einen unsren Lagerplatz begrenzenden Berg erstiegen hat, den steilsten, den wir noch zu erklimmen hatten. Glücklicherweise bedeckt ein fester Schnee die Wege und macht die Bewegung der schweren Bagage recht erträglich. Hätten wir den weichen Schnee und Morast vom Tage unseres Abmarsches von Rolla, so wäre es wohl eine Unmöglichkeit, die steilen Höhen und tiefen Schluchten zu überwinden, die wir gestern durchzogen und die heute vor uns liegen. Gleichwohl ging unser Marsch langsam genug vor sich; 9 Meilen betrug die ganze Strecke, die wir gestern zurücklegten.

Es war etwa 2 Uhr, als wir eine enge Schlucht betraten, bei deren Anblick mich unwillkürlich der Gedanke durchzuckte, wie radikal hier eine Colonne gleich der unsrigen weggefegt werden könnte.[42] Im Rücken und zu beiden Seiten von steilen, waldigen Höhen begrenzt, war sie gerade weit genug für unsere Straße und einen Bach, die sich durch den steinigen und buschigen Grund durchschlängelten. Und doch mühte sich einer dieser armen Missourischen Nomaden ab („Huscher" nennen wir Soldaten sie), längs einen der Bergabhänge, getrennt von uns durch den Bach und

---

[42] Diese Beobachtung, dass die „Colonne gleich der unsrigen weggefegt werden könnte", fehlt in der zweiten Fassung des Berichtes.

möglichst versteckt durch's Gesträuch durch, ein kleines Fuhrwerk mit seinem bischen fahrende Habe an uns vorbeizulaviren.[43]

Bald gerieth der lange Zug von Wagen in's Stocken, und indem wir uns durch denselben durchwanden, geriethen wir in einen bunten Knäuel von Wagen und Kanonen, Fußvolk und Reiterei, die alle in der trichterförmig erweiterten Schlucht sich drängten, die vor ihnen liegende Big Piney zu überschreiten. Das Fußvolk wurde auf den abgeladenen Bagagewagen hinübergeführt. Die Kanonen und besonders die zum Umwerfen bepackten Wagen machten dem geplagten Vieh oft lange und gewaltige Mühe, bis sie durch das eiskalte Wasser durchgestapft waren, so nahm dieser Flußübergeng den ganzen Rest des Tages in Anspruch.

Es war ein Theil der ersten Division und ein Theil unsrer eigenen, der 2ten Division, mit denen wir hier zusammentrafen. Die Menschenmasse war aber keineswegs so groß, als die Zahl der hier vertretenen Truppenkörper hätte vermuthen lassen. Es sind nicht mehr die vollzähligen Regimenter, die Illinois uns herüber gesandt hat; auch wir sind nicht mehr das stolze Regiment, das noch vor wenig Monaten als keines der geringsten unter der gewaltigen bunten Kriegerschaar Fremonts „auf nach Springfield" gezogen war. Witterung und Krankheit hatten uns allen mehr Abbruch gethan als der Feind, den wir nie zu Gesicht bekommen hatten.

Ende der 3. Manuskriptseite

Ein einziges und dazu nicht starkes Illionoisregiment hatte während der 2 1/2 Monate die wir bei Rolla im Winterquartier lagen, circa 170 in der fremden Erde begraben.

Um so wohlthätiger wirkt eine Scene wie ein solcher Flußübergang auf eine an Zahl geschwächte Schaar. Abgesehen von dem wirklich malerischen Anblick, den sie gewährt, übt sie sicherlich auch einen günstigen moralischen Einfluß. Der Geist – der langsam und oft vereinzelt vorwärts marschirenden Truppen wird durch die allgemeine Rührigkeit neu belebt und zugleich gekräftigt durch das Bewusstsein einer größeren, wohlorganisirten Masse anzugehören.[44]

Am jenseitigen Ufer der Big Piney dehnt sich, von einem Halbkreis waldiger Bergrücken begrenzt, ein weiter Thalgrund aus, in den sich die diesseitige trichgterförmige Schlucht erweitert und verläuft – unser Lagerplatz für den Rest des Tages und die Nacht.

Bei Waynesville, Febr. 5

Auf dem Pferde schreibe ich diesmal. Unsre Wagen sind wieder durch die weichen, tief eingeschnittenen Boden unseres Weges aufgehalten; bereits,

---

[43] "laviren" – "gewandt durch Schwierigkeiten hindurchwinden."
[44] Auch diese Beobachtung, dass „einer größeren, wohlorganisierten Maße anzugehören" den „Geist ... neu belebt" ist in der ersten Fassung nicht angeführt.

ist einer zum Opfer gefallen, und doch sind wir erst seit 5 Minuten aufgebrochen.

Unser Lager war etwa 2 Meilen über Waynesville hinaus aufgeschlagen. Ein angenehmer Marsch hatte uns dahin geführt, so angenehm wie wir selbst in der milden Jahreszeit wenige hatten. Nachdem wir die gestern genannte jähe Abdachung der die Big Piney begrenzenden Gebirgskette erstiegen und uns der Brand eines neune, großen Frainhauses – ein uns gewohntes Schauspiel – seinen Rauch nachgesandt hatte, führte uns die Straße ununterbrochen über den Rücken des Waldgebirges bis dicht vor Waynesville, welches in einem Thalkessel am Fuße der Berge gelegen ist. Zu beiden Seiten von größeren oder kleineren Schluchten und Gründen begrenzt, welche wieder in ebenso hohe, waldige Höhen auslaufen, bietet der Weg nicht die geringste Fernsicht, und zumal bei dem fast gänzlichen Mangel menschlicher Wohnungen möchte man sich vollständig, mitten in die Jagdgründe eines Indianerstammes versetzt glauben, wären nur wir nicht selber im Wege,[45] die dahinziehnden United States Soldaten, aus denen die Phantasie gewiß nicht wußte was machen in diesem einöden Missouri!

Waynesville selber ist eine sehr bescheidene Stadt; sie besteht aus einem Backsteinhaus, etwa 3 passablen Frainhäusern und verschiedenen Schandies und Barraken; eine Kirche habe ich nicht bemerkt und das zu meinem großen Erstaunen, da ich in einem amerikan. Flecken von einem Dutzend Häuser mindestens 3 Kirchen und doppelt so viele religiöse Gemeinschaften erwartet hätte. Das rothe, 2stöckige Backsteinhaus ist das Courthaus und liegt in der Mitte eines außerordentlich großen, freien Platzes, welcher wohl andeuten soll, für wie viel Häuser hier noch Raum ist, um aus Waynesville eine Stadt zu machen. Übrigens schienen

Ende der 4. Manuskriptseite
(Februar 5.)

im gegenwärtigen Augenblick immer noch mehr Häuser vorhanden zu sein als Bewohner; denn außer einigen alten Negerweibern und Hunden[46] kamen uns nur wenige zu Gesicht. Während einer viertelstündigen Rast, die hier gemacht wurde, waren die meisten Officiere bedacht, eines Mittagessens oder wenigstens einer Schale Kaffe habhaft zu w. Mit e. Freunde[47] benützte ich die Zeit, um das Courthaus zu inspizieren. Alle Thüren waren aufgesperrt oder eingeschlagen, kein Mensch im ersten Stockwerk zu finden, wo in 2 Zimmern die Archive aufbewart waren, dagegen um so mehr hohe und lange Fächer, gefüllt mit jenen unvermeidlichen, in gelbes Leder gebundenen

---

[45] „wären nur wir uns nicht selber im Wege" mit dem abwertenden Hinweis auf Missouri fehlt auch in der ersten Fassung.

[46] Auch dieser Hinweis fehlt in der ursprünglichen Fassung.

[47] Der Hinweis auf den Freund, mit dem das „Courthaus" inspiziert wurde, fehlt in der ersten Fassung.

Büchern, welche die Basis eines jeden amerikan. Gemeinwesens bilden. Trotz meiner angeborenen Antipathie gegen solche ledernen Bücher durchwühlte ich diese Archive mit einem Eifer, daß ein Zuschauer nichts anders vermuthet haben würde, als suche ich nach staatsgefährl. Schriften oder wenigstens nach dem Census der hiesigen Bürger, wer die höchsten Taxes bezahle und die meisten Nigger füttere.[48] Ich suchte vergeblich nach einer Karte von Missouri. Im obern Stockwerk trafen wir eine unerwartete Gesellschaft, eine Gruppe Artilleristen, die hinter ihrer Batterie zurückgeblieben waren, nicht mehr wußten, wo sie hingekommen wäre, und nun beabsichtigten, in ruhsamer Eil sie gelegentlich wieder irgendwo aufzufinden. Sie ruhten sich hier aus, um ein Kaminfeuer auf dem Boden ausgestreckt, und vertrieben sich damit die Zeit, daß einer dem anderen auf den im Archive vorgefundenen Blanks Anweisungen austellte auf so und so viel Acres Land in Pulaski County.

Etwa 2 Meilen weiter schlugen wir uner Nachtlager auf. Am Wege dahin war ein Secessionist so unglücklich seine Farm stehen zu haben und büßte dafür seinen ganzen Vorrath an Korn und Heu ein, welche mit großer Behendigkeit aus seiner Schune in die Camps unsrer Truppen gemovt[49] wurden. Ebendaher brachte Abends einer meiner Leute, dessen Blutdürstigkeit sich sogar auf secessionistisches Vieh erstreckte, einen gewaltigen Hahn. Ich hätte denselben eigentlich wieder an seinen Master ausliefern sollen. Allein da die Dunkelheit schon hereingebrochen war, blieb mir nichts anders übrig, als das Corpus delicti zum Tode durch Beil oder Säbel und zur Sättigung meines hungrigen Magens zu verdauen. Doch ein rächendes Schicksal sollte mich für eine solche Aneignung fremden Eigenthums bestrafen, indem es meine schönen Hoffnungen auf ein delicates Abendessen zerstörte. Mochte nun meine Unerfahrenheit in d. Kochkunst die Schuld tragen od das Alter des Thieres od sein rebellische Ursprung – genug, der Braten war so zäh, daß ich nicht mehr Geschmack daran finden konnte als an den ledernen Büchern im Courthaus.

Bei Lebanon, Febr. 6

Zwei Tagesmärsche haben uns nach dem Städtchen Lebanon, unseren nächsten Bestimmungsort, gebracht. Auf einer weiten, mit Präriegras und niederm Gesträuch überdeckten Heide nur hie und wieder von einer Gruppe Bäume unterbrochen, hat unre Division ihr Lager aufgeschlagen. Auf demselben Boden, aber zur andern Seite der Straße liegt die erste Division. Es ist dies der angenehmste Lagerplatz, den wir noch je gehabt, eine trockene,

---

[48] Dieser „Eifer" wurde in der ersten Fassung nicht erwähnt.
[49] Der Autor übernimmt in dieser zweiten Fassung einige Anglizismen: „Blanks" (vermutlich blanke Formulare, die es auszufüllen gilt), „gemovt" (deutsches part. perf. von *move* im Sinne von *befördern*)

sonnige Heide, durchflossen von einem kleinen Bache. Aus dem Gras und Gebüsch ragen, gleich Zuckerhüten, unsre

Ende der 5. Manuskriptseite

weißen, hoch zugespitzten Zelte hervor, und in naher Entfernung gewahrt man die Dächer von Lebanon. Wir richten uns bereits zu einem etwas längern Aufenthalt ein, diese Rast kommt uns nicht wenig erwünscht. Denn es waren 2 mühsame Tagemärsche, die uns von Waynesville hieher gebracht. Der erste derselben hatte uns über ein Hügelland, weit niedriger als das zuvor durchzogene, bie einbrechender Dunkelheit zur Gasconade geführt. Kaum hatten wir dieselbe überschritten und an ihren steilen Ufern unsre Zelte aufgeschlagen, als uns ein heftiger Regen überfiel, welcher die ganze Nacht anhielt und Lagerplatz und Straßen in Moräste umwandelte.[50]

Dazu kam den andern Morgen, als wir frühzeitig aufbrachen, eine äußerst empfindliche Kälte, wie sie in Gebirgsgegenden auf Regen zu folgen pflegt, so daß dieser Marsch der mühseligste wurde, den wir noch zu bestehen hatten. Mir für meine Person stellte sich die mießliche Wahl, entweder zu Fuß mich durch fußhohen Koth, Schnee und Wasser durchzuarbeiten od. zu Pferde mir die nassen Füße steif frieren zu laßen. Ich wählte das Letztere, war aber herzlich froh, nach einem 2 stündigen Marsche ein Blockhaus an d. Straße zu finden, worin an der behaglichen Wärme eines Kaminfeuers meine erfrorenen Glieder neu belebt wurden und unter Plaudern und Rauchen ein Stündchen verstrich, worauf es auch draußen wärmer zu werden begann und ich in scharfem Trabe unserm Regimente nacheilte. Der Farmer, welcher dies Blockhaus bewohnte, war ein Unionsmann und bedeutete dies durch ein kleines Fähnchen, welches vor seiner Thüre hing. Deshalb war auch ein Cavallerist als Wache vor sein Gehöft gestellte, um ihn, wirksamer als jenes Fähnchen, vor einer zu nahen Berührung mit den vorbeiziehenden Unionstruppen zu sichern. Es waren daher nur eingie wenige unsrer Officiere, welche den Mann um Erlaubniss baten, an seinem Kamin zu sitzen, darunter an meiner Seite ein ältlicher Mann mit den hellen, verständigen Augen und der scharf geschnittenen, weder schönen noch häßlichen Physiognomie eines Yankee. Gesprächig, wie Alle, begann er sogleich mit mir zu plaudern. Er war aus Ohio, kein Soldat, obwohl er den blauen Soldatenmantel trug, und herzlich froh, es nicht zu sein; aber er hatte einen Sohn bei der zu unserer Division gehörigen 2. Ohiobatterie, und dieser lag krank an der Auszehrung im Spital zu Rolla, und der Militärarzt hatte ihn aufgegeben. Diesen zu sehn, war mein Nachbar hier nach Missouri gekommen, und um seine Entlassung vom Dienst auszuwirken, begleitete er uns nach Lebanon.[51]

---

[50] Der Hinweis auf die erste Übernachtung bei Waynesville fehlt in der ersten Fassung.
[51] Dieses Gespräch mit dem älteren „Yankee" aus Ohio fehlt in der ersten Fassung.

Auf meine Frage, wie ihm dies Missouri gefalle, schüttelte er lächelnd den Kopf und meinte, es wäre das armseligste Land, was er noch gesehn; er sei jetzt kaum 4 Wochen hier, aber er wolle herzlich froh sein, wenn er zu seiner Familie nach Ohio zurückkehren könne. Wie schön sei es nicht am Eriesee, wo er wohne!

„Denkt Ihr nicht, es sei das schönste Land der Welt?" – fragte mein anderer Nachbar, ein Schweizer.

„Gewiß ist es das schönste" – antwortete mit naiver Zuversicht der Amerikaner und begann zur Bestätigung seiner Aussage, uns ein begeistertes Bild von seiner malerischen Heimath am Eriesee zu entwerfen.

Seiner Erzählung folgte mit wehmüthigen Blicken die Farmersfrau, welche samt ihren Kindern mit uns im Raum saß. Als wir uns mit der Frage an sie wandten, wie sie eigentlich in diesem Lande ihr

Ende der 6. Manuskriptseite

Leben machte,[52] und wovon sie namentlich in der gegenwärtigen Zeit zu leben hätten, füllten sich ihre Augen mit Thränen und gab sie uns folg. Auskunft: Früher hätten sie ihr Leben gut gemacht und mehr als das. Sie hätten Waizen und Welschkorn gepflanzt und es 25 Meilen weit nach einer Mühle gefahren oder „an Stock"[53] gelassen und gelegentlich an vorbeiziehende Händler verkauft. Außerdem hätten sie Pferde, Rinder und Schweine gezogen. Für rohes Schweinefleisch erhielten sie noch vor einem Jahr 5 Cents das Pfund, für ein Joch Ochsen 60-70 Thaler.[54] Aber jetzt freilich sei dies alles anders geworden. Schweinefleisch ist nur noch 2 einhalb Cents werth; für ein Joch Ochsen gibt man nicht mehr als 25-30 $, und man muß froh sein, wenn man überhaupt nur Absatz findet. Sie wüßten gar nicht mehr, wovon leben, hätten sie nicht Vieles versteckt gehabt. Denn die Secessionisten, welche 1500 Mann stark in ihrer Gegend gelegen, hätten ihnen alles fortgenommen, was zu finden war. Auch von den Unionstruppen, die schon wiederholt hier vorbeigezogen, wäre ihnen sehr vieles genommen worden; für das meiste hätten sie zwar Anweisungen an die Regierung erhalten, oft genug sei dies aber auch unterlassen worden. Immerhin konnten sie sich noch glücklich schätzen im Vergleich zu vielen andern Unionsleuten ihrer Nachbarschaft, denen Alles und jedes genommen worden, so daß sie jetzt in der bittersten Noth lebten.

Wir lauschten theilnahmsvoll der Schilderung dieser Frau; wir wußten, daß sie die reine Wahrheit sprach. Denn wir hatten selber zu jenen Truppen gehört, denen als dem Nachtrapp der Unionsarmee, die den Südwesten Missouris aufgab und räumte, ein langer Zug flüchtiger Unionsleute sich

---

[52] Anglizismus: *to make a living*
[53] „in stock", vermutlich: *auf Lager*
[54] Vermutlich bezieht sich „Thaler" auf *Dollar*

angeschlossen, die der menschenfreundlichen Aufforderung Siegels, der ihnen seinen Schutz angeboten, gefolgt waren, um jenseits des Mississippi im friedlichen, fruchtbaren Illinois sich eine neue Heimstätte zu gründen, mittellos und mitten im Winter, während ihre alte Heimath mit Gut und Besitzthum der Rache des auf dem Fuße folgenden Feindes preiß gegeben werde. Und seither, während unsres Aufenthaltes in Rolla hatten wir Gelegenheit, Hunderte solcher armer Flüchtlinge zu sehn, welche nach dieser äußersten Eisenbahnstation des Südwestens geeilt kamen.

An dieses Elend durch die Erzählung der Missourischen Farmersfrau erinnert, wandte ich mich, im Aufstehen begriffen, nochmals an den Mann aus Ohio, von dem derselbe Krieg die Gesundheit und bald auch das Leben eines Kindes gefordert.

„Was haltet Ihr von diesem Krieg in Missouri?" – fragte ich ihn.

„Ich begreife nicht, wie die Regierung so viel Geld ausgeben mag für dies arme Missouri" – war die Antwort des Yankee.

Ende der 7. Manuskriptseite

Tagebuch eines Missouri Freiwilligen
während des gegenwärtigen Feldzugs. (Fortsetzung)

In Benton Co., Arkansas, Febr. 20.

Vierzehn Tage sind verstrichen, seit die letzten Zeilen unsern Kreuzzug durch Missouri beschrieben. (Man frage den ersten besten Missourier, ob es nicht ein Zug gewesen, der Kreuz[55] genug gebracht.) Seither haben wir unsre nächste Aufgabe gelöst; Missouri ist von feindlichen Truppen gesäubert. Diese Zeilen sind bereits auf dem Boden von Arkansas geschrieben.

Es war eine angenehme Rast, die paar Tage, die uns in Lebanon vergönnt waren. Unter einer milden Frühlingssonne wurde hier gewirthaftet, gebraten und gebacken, wie es an Fest- und Ruhetagen im häuslichen Leben zu geschehn pflegt. Unsere Jungens durchstrichen mit ihren Büchsen die Umgegend nach allen Seiten; sie gingen auf die Jagd, sagten sie. Aber die eigentlichen Ansiedler unsrer Heide, eine schwere Menge Kaninchen, die bei unsrer Ankunft, als echte Missouri „Huscher", das Weite gesucht, lieferten nur eine geringe Zugabe zu unsrer Tafel. Die eigentliche Beute bestand in Schweinen, Schafen und Federvieh jeder Art, die im Busche herum, wohin sie der Sicherheit-wegen getrieben worden, oder im Gehöfte vor den Augen des Eigenthümers weggeschossen oder eingefangen wurden, mochten nun die Weiber darüber weinen und die Männer sich noch so sehr bemühn, darzuthun, daß sie Unionsleute wären – eine immer sehr zweifelhafte Behauptung, zumal wenn aus irgend einer Thüre das halb furchtsame, halb schadenfroh grinsende Gesicht eines zerlumpten Negerweibes hervorguckte

---

[55] Vermutlich im Sinne von „Last" oder „Leid".

– und mit verbissenen Grimme erklären, dass es ihr Letztes sei und sie nicht wüßten, wovon sich und ihre Familie ernähren, wenn ihnen auch dies noch genommen würde. Letztere Erklärung klang schon glaubwürdiger; denn wir mußten uns fast wundern, noch so viel in diesem schon so lange vom Kriege heimgesuchten Lande zu finden. Aber der Soldat hat kein mitleidig Herz, auch nicht für das Elend eines so armen Volkes wie das, dem wir in Missouri begegneten, – ein Volk, das mit schwerer Arbeit der Wildnis das Brod und eine Blockhütte für sein armseliges Dasein abringen, und dessen einziger Reichtum in einem großen Kindersegen zu bestehen scheint. Mit dem Ausgehen des mitgeführten Proviants oder mit dem Überdruß an demselben – d. h. sobald

Ende der 1. Manuskriptseite (der Fortsetzung)

irgendwo ein Hahn schreit oder ein Schaf blöckt – erwacht die Raublust, und ist diese erst im Soldaten erwacht, so kennt er keine Grenzen mehr; er nimmt nicht nur, was er braucht – und das wäre sehr verzeihlich – sondern schleppt fort und schießt zusammen, was für ihn keinen Werth hat und er wieder fortwirft oder unberührt liegen läßt, und was er nicht fortschleppen kann, zerstört er wenigstens. So war es auf unserem letzten Zuge nach Springfield geschehn. Noch stehen in meiner Erinnerung die jammernden Gestalten zweier Männer „am Grabe ihrer Habe", eines Landmannes, dessen reiche Schafherde zerfleischt die Prairie deckte, zusammengesäbelt von einem Truppe übermüthiger Cavalleristen, und eines weinenden Schusters, dessen Schusterwerkzeuge, die einzige Quelle für den Unterhalt seiner Familie, ihm, dem deutschen Unionsmanne, von einem deutschen Soldaten schonungslos vor den Augen weggestohlen wurden.

Es macht einen eigenthümlichen Eindruck, eine todte Stadt zu sehn. Auf unserem Marsch durch Missouri bot jede Ortschaft mehr oder weniger diesen Anblick, aber keine mehr als Lebanon. Lebanon, das äußerste Städtchen in der Richtung gegen Rolla, welches der Feind besetzt gehalten, und in dessen Nähe ihn noch bei unsrer Ankunft die Gerüchte seine Hauptmacht zu einer entscheidenden Schlacht concentriren ließen, ist hoch gelegen und stellt, abgesehn von der Geschäftsstraße, einen Haufen über eine rauhe, unebene Landfläche unregelmäßig hingewürfelter Frainhäuser vor. Sonst mochte es 800 - 1000 Einwohner zählen; gegenwärtig suchte man fast ebenso vergeblich nach seinen Bürgern wie nach Cedern. Ich gab mir auch wirklich Mühe, eine hiesige Familie aufzufinden, um über den Feind und ihr eigenes Schicksal während der letzten Kriegszeit Einiges zu vernehmen. Aber wo ich in ein Haus hineinblickte, die ganze Hauptstraße entlang, fand ich überall als Insassen der Stores und Officen[56] Cavalleristen, die rauchend und plaudernd um die Ofen gruppiert oder auf dem Counter ausgestreckt waren,

---

[56] „Stores und Officen" vermutlich: *Geschäfte und Büros*

während in den ehemaligen Waaren Fächern Säbel, Pferdebürsten und dergl herumlagen und in den anstossenden Zimmern oder Nebengebäuden die Pferde ihre Ställe gefunden hatten. In den Höfen oder zwischen den Häusern stand vereinzelt ein Officierszelt und an den Fencen waren frisch abgezogene Schafsbälge zum Trocknen ausgehängt. Wäre es Sitte, daß amerikanische Städte Wappen führten, Lebanon könnte wahrlich keine bessere Wahl treffen, als so einen ausgenommenen

Ende der 2. Manuskriptseite

Schafsbalk in sein Wappen zu setzen.

Ich wandte auf meiner Entdeckungsreise, die Schritten einem hübschen Landhause am Ende des Städtchens zu und fragte einen davorstehenden Cavalleristen nach seinen Bewohnern. „General Siegel wohnt hier" – war die Antwort, und als ich auf ein zweites hinwies, hieß es: „Das ist das Hauptquartier des General Curtis." – ...[57] „Schon gut, danke für die Auskunft" – unterbrach ich und wandte mich mit meinem Begleiter weg, mit einer gleichgültig ernsten Miene, so nahe mir auch das Lachen stand; mein Begleiter war unser Feldkaplan.

Auf unserem Heimwege waren wir endlich so glücklich, eine Famile von Eingeborenen zu entdecken. Sie bestand aus einer Frau und einigen Kindern, die sich mit ein paar Cavalerieofficieren in die zwei Zimmer des Häuschens getheilt hatten. Wir setzten uns zu der Frau an's Kamin und bemühten uns, Einiges von Interesse aus ihr herauszukriegen, aber mit gerigem Erfolg. Wir fragten sie ob sie auch noch ihr Leben machen könne und wie; was denn aus den übrigen Einwohnern Lebanons geworden sei; ob die Sezeßionisten, die hier gelegen, Missourier oder südliche Truppen gewesen wären – auf alle Fragen folgte die stereotype Antwort: „ich weiß nicht" – dieselbe Antwort, die wir mit seltenen Ausnahmen immer erhielten, wo wir ähnliche Fragen an Missourier richteten. Nur so viel konnten wir von einem dabeistehenden Jungen erfahren, daß etwa vor 18 Tagen die feindlichen Truppen Lebanon verlassen hätten, daß es nur etwa 800 Reiter gewesen wären, daß sie von befreundeten Familien beherbergt worden und sich Niemand über ihre Aufführung beklagt hätte. Als wir die Frau nach ihrem Manne fragten, erwiederte sie, er sei bei der nördlichen Armee. Wir wußten damit genug. Auf unserem letzten Zuge nach Springfield wurde uns überall, wo wir uns nach den Männern erkundigten, der Bescheid: sie seien bei General Siegel. Damals marschierten wir getrennt von Siegel's Division.

---

[57] Die folgenden sechs Zeilen sind durchgestrichen; die ersten vier sind zur Gänze unleserlich, die letzten zwei lauten: „Schon gut, danke für die Auskunft" – unterbrach ich und wandte mich mit meinem Begleiter weg, mit einer gleichgültig ernsten Miene, so nahe mir auch das Lachen stand; mein Begleiter war unser Feldkaplan.

Montag Morgens – Februar 10. – verließen sämtliche Truppen Lebanon. Es waren vier Divisionen, die sich hier vereinigt hatten. Die erste und zweite, unter Siegel's Commando, diesmal Curtis als dem Oberbefehlshaber der ganzen Armee an der Spitze, marschirten zusammen, die dritte und 4. Division unter Jefferson

Ende der 3. Manuskriptseite

Davis aus Indiana auf einem andern Wege, um in Springfield wieder mit uns zusammenzutreffen. Die milde Frühlingssonne, die uns in Lebanon zum ersten Mal nach den rauhen Wintertagen der letzten Wochenbegrüßt hatte, ließ uns glauben, daß Winter und Kälte jetzt hinter uns lagen, je näher dem sonnigen Süden wir kämen, und leicht und wohlgemuth, wie Wanderer im Monat Mai, schritten wir über das buschige Hügelland. Ein verhältnismäßig guter Fahrweg brachte uns gegen Abend des zweiten Tages nach dem Städtchen Marshfield. Hier hatten noch am Morgen vor unserer Ankunft die feindlichen Vorposten des Feindes gestanden, und von da an bis in das Lager in Arkansas, wo wir gegenwärtig liegen, glaubten wir täglich, ihm selber begegnen zu müssen.

Ein buntes Gewirr von Menschen und Wagen bezeichnete am folgenden Morgen den Aufbruch der beiden Divisionen, welcher diesmal dicht nebeneinander ihr Nachtlager gehabt hatten, und es dauerte eine lange Weile, bis sich der Knäuel gelöst und die Truppen mit ihren Wagenzügen in Bewegung gesetzt. „So viel Menschen hat Marshfield noch nie beisammen gesehn" – bemerkte uns im Verbeiziehn ein Bürger mit erzwungenem Lächeln, während er sicherlich im Stillen uns einen Fluch nachsandte, wenn er auf die rauchenden Trümmer einiger noch während des verzögerten Abmarsches niedergebrannten Häuser und durch die zerschlagenen Fensterscheiben in die vielen verlassenen Wohnungen blickte, in denen zertrümmert worden, was zurückgeblieben war. Als wir schon zum Abmarsch aufgestellt waren, kam unser General vor die Fronte geritten und verlas uns die Siegesnachricht von Fort Henry. Ein frohes Hurrah erwiderte, und mit derselben Siegeszuversicht ging es dem Feinde entgegen, wie einst unter Fremont demselben Feinde gegenüber.

Das vor uns liegende Hügelland begann ein wilderes Aussehn zu gewinnen, und Nachmittags kamen wir wieder in ein wirkliches Waldegebirge mit steilen Abhängen und Schluchten. Die Straße war rauh und durch die schweren Geschütze tief eingeschnitten, der Boden weich, of so morastig, daß sich unser Fußvolk auf weite Strecken einzeln in den Feldern oder durch den Wald einen Weg suchen mußte. Dazu kam daß der Train der Siegel'schen Division anfangs vor uns ging, bis wir ungeduldig über die beständige Verzögerung denselben passirten. So wurde der Marsch zu einem äußerst langwirigen; bald blieb ein Wagen stecken und mußte durch Vorspann unter unglaublichen Flüchen und Hieben auf das gequälte Vieh wieder flott gemacht werden, bald brach eines zusammen und wurde bei Seite geschafft und abgeladen.

Ende der 4. Manuskriptseite

Je weiter wir vorwärts schritten, desto größer wurde die Spannung, womit wir auf das Erscheinen einer Ordonanz oder das Knallen der Geschütze harrten, welche uns das erste Zusammentreffen mit dem Feinde verkünden sollten. Eine auffallende Veränderung läßt sich an einem solchen Tage unter den Truppen beobachten. Statt sich, wie gewohnt, nach rechts oder links zu zerstreuen, hinter der Colonne zurückzubleiben oder singend, raisonirend und späßetreibend vorwärts zu marschiren, blieben sie heute alle schön beisammen und schritten mäuschenstill, nur darauf bedacht, ihre Büchsen in Bereitschaft zu halten, ihres Weges dahin.

Es war gegen 4 Uhr Nachmittags, wir durchzogen gerade einen breiten waldigen Bergrücken, als ich vor uns, wie aufsteigende Nebel, unheimliche schwarze Wolken erhoben und die sich neigende Sonne verdunkelte. Eine immer glühnderwerdende Hitze, je näher wir kamen, ein brenzlicher Geruch, ein lautes Knistern und Prasseln verriethen uns, daß der Wald vor uns in Brand gerathen sei. Durch einen Rauch, der uns kaum zwei Schritte weit unsern Weg erkennen ließ und unsre Augen aufs Empfindlichste schmerzte und kaum offen zu halten erlaubte, und eine unerträgliche Gluth eilten wir, die Strecke hinter uns zu kriegen, wo im Umfang einer Meile, zu beiden Seiten der Straße, die Flammen begierig um sich griffen, indem sie der Wind hastig nach allen Seiten über das dürre Laub und Gras vorwärts trieb und sie an den niedern Bäumen und Sträuchern, aus denen die hiesigen Wälder bestehn, leicht und zierlich, gleich Eichhörnchen, heraufglitten und von einem Ast zu einem nahen andern hüpften. Wir hatten heute schon zwei brennende Waldstrecken durchschritten; an der zweiten zeigte sich abseits und halb versteckt ein Bäuerlein, welches, gleich furchtsam vor uns, die wir ihm wehren möchten, wie vor den Flammen, einen langen Graben zu ziehn bemüht war, um dadurch dem Feuer eine Grenze zu setzen und es von seiner nahen Farm abzuhalten. Der letzte war der bedeutendste Brand der Art gewesen, seine Urheber konnten nur Soldaten der Siegelschen Division sein, die sich diesen sträflichen Spaß erlaubten, unbekümmert um ihre nachfolgenden Kameraden und deren schmerzende Augen.

Mit eintreten der Dunkelheit erreichten wir eine lange Schlucht, die unsern Weg kreuzte. Hier sollte unre Division für diese Nacht rasten, während diejenige Siegels noch etwas weiter zog.

Ende der 5. Manuskriptseite

Da unsre Wagen weit zurückgeblieben waren, so nahm auch die Einrichtung des Lagers wenig Zeit in Anspruch; sein Abendbrot fand jeder in seinem Brodsack, falls noch Etwas darin übrig war, und seine Schlafstelle bereitete er sich auf dem steinigen Boden aus zusammengetragenen Laube.

Wir hatten uns aber nicht lange auf dem harten Bette zur Ruhe gelegt, als wir durch drei sich rasch folgende Kanonenschüsse aufgeschreckt und durch das Wirbeln unsrer Trommeln zur Sammlung gerufen wurden. Mit einem wahren Freudenjauchzen sprangen unsre Jungen zu den Gewehren, und so rüstig und unverdrossen nahmen sie den Marsch wieder auf, als hätten sie in einem langen Schlafe von dem eben bestandenen ausgeruht. Doch hatten wir nicht viel mehr als eine Meile Wegs hinter uns, als Contreordre erschien und wir mit Zurücklassung dreier Companien, welche den Vorpostendienst zu versehn hatten, zu unsern Laubbetten zurückkehrten.

Nach kurzer Ruhe traten wir um 4 Uhr des folgenden Morgens wieder an. Die Tornister wurden zusammengeworfen und eine Wache dabei zurückgelassen; nur seinen Brodsack und eine Decke hatte der Soldat umgehängt. Es war noch Nacht; doch der sinkende Mond, dessen Richtung wir folgten, beleuchtete matt unsern Weg über das Waldgebirge, und eine frostige Kälte trieb uns rasch vorwärts. Wir hatten etwa 4 Meilen zurückgelegt, als eine Menge verglimmender Feuer, die auf eine weite Strecke über die Felder einer einsam gelegenen Farm ausgestreut waren, sowie die Masse zurückgelassener Wagen und an den Seiten der Straße einzelne Haufen von Tornister, Pauken und Instrumenten uns die Stelle bezeichneten, wo Siegels Division, die eben aufgebrochen war, ihr Nachtlager gehalten hatte.

Hier war es auch, wo vorigen Abend die äussersten Vorposten des Feindes, eine Abtheilung Cavallerie, unsre vordersten Truppen mit einigen Flintenschüssen begrüßt hatte, und durch jene drei Kartätschenschüsse von unsrer Seite, unter Zurücklassung einiger Todter und Verwundeter verjagt worden waren.

Bald brachten uns einzelne zurückkehrende Reiter die weniger unerwartete als unerwünschte Kunde, daß die gesammte feindliche Armee Springfield geräumt habe und auf dem Rückzug begriffen sei. So zogen wir ohne Schwertstreich denselben Morgen in Springfield ein, unsre Division zum zweiten, Siegel zum vierten Mal. Am 13. November hatten wir ihm den Rücken gekehrt, den 13. Februar, also gerade drei Monate später, kehrten wir heute wieder ein.

Springfield, die Hauptstadt des Südwestens, ist ein hübsches, freundliches Städtchen mit manchem stattlichen Frainhaus und ein paar großen Backsteinhäusern, auf einer Höhe gelegen, die sich nach einer Seite in einen Wiesengrund abdacht. Vier Landstraßen treffen sich unter rechten Winkeln auf dem viereckigen Marktplatz, in dessen Mitte das alte Courthaus stund,
Ende der 6. Manuskriptseite

welches bei unserem ersten Einzuge niederbrannte. Es erwuchs daraus kein Schaden, auch blieb die Veranlassung des Brandes unbekannt. Springfield hat dadurch einen freien geräumigen Platz gewonnen an dessen Seite sich das kaum vollendete neue Courthaus, ein großes Backsteingebäude, erhebt.

Noch immer wehte darauf die gelbe Hospitalflagge; unter ihrem Schutze und unter der Pflege eines zurückgebliebenen Assistenzarztes hatten wir hier letztes Spätjahr die Verwundeten von Wilsons Creek wieder gefunden, während dieselbe Flagge ein zweites großes Backsteinhaus als das Spital der zurückgelassenen Kranken oder verwundeten Sezessionisten bezeichntete. Vor unserm Rückzuge waren unsere sämtlichen Invaliden fortgeschafft worden. Als Hospital der Sezessionisten trafen wir diesmal das neue Courthaus wieder.

So hatte die gelbe Flagge die beiden andern Flaggen überdauert, in Springfield und fast in ganz Südmissouri, jene gelbe Flagge, welche das menschliche Elend andeutet, den neutralen Boden, wo der scharfe Hake in das Fleisch des Freundes wie des Feindes gleich kalt und unbarmherzig einschneidet. Ja wohl war es menschliches Elend, was jeder der feindlichen Brüder hinterlassen; menschliches Elend, was sich auf den Gesichtern der wenigen Einwohner ausdrückte, die wir in den Straßen Springfields gewahr wurden. Hier hätte ein Physiognomiker ein reiches Gebiet gehabt, aus den gemischten Zügen die so geheim und doch so hei sprudelnden Regungen des Herzens zu deuten. Neugierde, das Erbstück des Amerikaners, Verwunderung, ob es möglich sei, daß wir wieder an diesem Platze einzögen, den wir drei Monate lang dem Feinde überlassen hatten, hie und da ein unglückliches Lächeln, unglücklich, weil offenbar eine zu erzwungene und darum auch vergeblich veruchte Freudenbezeugung, als Grundzug aber, der alle andern beherrschte, Furcht und Schrecken – das sprachen, jedem leserlich, die Züge der paar Leutchen, die sich ängstlich vor einigen Häusern zeigten oder vorüberhuschten, dieser Leutchen, die heute uns und gestern unsere Feinde durch ihre kläglichen oder freundlichen Mienen und Worte um Schonung flehten für ihr Bischen Habe, die zu klein war, als daß sie dieselbe hätten im Stiche lassen und fliehen können.

Springfield war ein menschenleerer Ort zu nennen, als wir es das letzte Spätjahr zum ersten Mal sahen; noch weit leerer sah es heute drein. An der Straße, auf der wir einzogen,
Ende der 7. Manuskriptseite

lag dicht am Beginn der Häuserreihen ein mit zerbissenen Bäumen bewachsenes Feld, welches sich auf den ersten Blick als Lagerplatz einer Abtheilung Cavallerie zu erkennen gab. Gut ausgehöhlte Baumstämme zeugten von der Sorgsamkeit der Reiter für ihre Pferde, eine gute Menge zerstreut herumliegenden oder noch gehäuften Welschkorns, einige große eiserne Kessel und andere Geräthschaften von einem erst kürzlich und eilig erfolgten Aufbruche. Viele Häuser und Scheunen an dieser Straße standen leer und offen; ihre Böden warn mit Strich belegt; offenbar hatten darin Truppen gelegen, und mit großer Wahrscheinlichkeit wurde daraus geschlossen, daß es die Wohnungen geflüchteter Unionsleute waren. Viele andere, darunter sehr stattliche, mit den bekannten kleinen Frainhäuschen, den Negerwohnungen, in einiger Entfernung zu beiden Seiten hinter ihnen, waren gleichfalls unbewohnt, oder es war wenigstens Niemand sichtbar, aber geschlossen und sichtlich von jeder feindseligen Hand bisher unberührt, sie wurden als Häuser von Sezessionisten gedeutet.

Ohne den geringsten Verzug zogen wir durch die Stadt und auf den Marktplatz. Eben wurde eine Unzahl Gefangener vorübergeführt; ohne Waffen oder irgendwelche Kriegerische Abzeichen sahen sie aus wie gewöhnliche Farmersbuben. Wir liessen hier eine Companie für die Provostguarde zurück, von deren Wirksamkeit die bald folgenden Ereignisse einen sehr unklaren Begriff gaben; und zogen, ohne weitern Halt, auf der gerade entgegengesetzten Straße zur Stadt hinaus. Dabei kamen wir an einem großen einstöckigen Hause vorüber, welches mit Einem Schlage die mancherlei Erinnerungen, die das Wiedersehn Sprigfields erweckte, zu einem lebendigen Bilde vereingt, vor die Seele treten ließ. Es war das ehemalige Hauptquartier Fremonts.

Welch buntes Gemälde kriegerischen Lebens bot einst dies Haus und seine Umbegung; nie werde ich lebhafter an Wallensteins Lager erinnert als bei diesem Anglick. Da trafen sich und wogten durcheinander Krieger von allen Waffengattungen, Truppen aus den meisten westlichen Staaten, von Ohio bis Nabraska, selbst eine Companie berittener Indianer, die Lanc aus Kansas mitgebracht hatte, hohe, bewegliche Gestalten, mit ihrer dunkeln Gesichtsfarbe, den langen Haaren und spitzen Hüten von Weitem fast wie Calabresen anzusehn, eine gute Zahl alter europäischer Officiere aus aller Herren Länder besonders aus der deutschen und der ungarischen Revolution, auch ein paar junge Italiener von Garibaldis ehemaliger Südarmee und dabei nicht zu vergessen, die vielen alten deutschen Soldaten und Unterofficiere, die als Cavalleristen und Artilleristen sich wieder so leicht und stolz im langentbehrten Saddel bewegten. Auf der andern Seite der Straße hatte Fremonts Leibgarde

Ende der 8. Manuskriptseite

ihr Lager, schmucke, schlanke, jugendliche Reiter. Sie hatten ein Recht, stolz zu sein; denn sie waren die einzigen von der ganzen großen Armee, denen vergönnt gewesen, durch ihr kühnes Reiterstückchen, wie dieser großartige Krieg wenige wird aufweisen können, dem Feinde und noch mehr den Freunden im Osten und der übrigen Welt zu beweisen, welcher Geist damals die westliche Armee beseelte, und was sie hätte ausführen können.

Aber den Göttern im weißen Olymp hatte es anders gefallen. Unser Wallenstein ward von uns genommen. Ein Anderer kam mit dem verhängnisvollen Brief in der Tasche, ein Schriftgelehrter von West-Point. Zu spät nach dem Plane Fremonts, wonach er einige Tage früher hier hätte eintreffen sollen, um mit den übrigen Divisionen insgesamt auf den Feind loszurücken und den entscheidenden Schlag zu führen, kam er immer noch zu früh für uns, die wir lieber ohne ihn gekämpft, als mit ihm retirirt[58] hätten. Es dürfte schwer halten, sich eine Vorstellung zu machen von der Umwandlung, welche die Ereignisse weniger Tage in der Stimmung unsrer Truppen hervorzurufen im Stande waren. Kurz nach unrer Ankunft in Springfield wurde einst um Mitternacht Generalmarsch geblasen. Tornister, Zelte, alle Baggage zurückgelassen un vorwärts! – lautete der Befehl; die Stunde der täglich erwarteten Schlacht schien gekommen zu sein. Da hätte man aber die Kampfeslust und die Siegeszuversicht, die aus allen Gesichtern hervorleuchtete, sehn sollen. Ein Mißgeschick unsrer Waffen galt für eine Unmöglichkeit, an die gar nicht gedacht wurde. Wer da durch die Reihen der Zelte wandelte und die Gruppen plaudernder Soldaten belauschte, traf nur Jubel und Entschlossenheit, nicht Ein Wort oder Gesicht, was Furcht verrieth. Einen oder zwei Abende später konnte man dieselben Gruppen um ihre Feuer stehen finden; ihre Reden wurden noch weit lauter und hitziger geführt; aber Entrüstung, Enttäuschung und Rathlosigkeit, was zu thun sei und was aus alledem werden soll – waren darin ausgesprochen. Noch verstimmter, wo möglich, und unschlüssiger waren die Officiere. Eine unheimliche gedrückte Stimmung, wie trübe schwüle Gewitterluft, hatte mit Einemmal die Gemüther befallen. „Zum Teufel war der Spiritus – der Gehorsam war geblieben."

Was folgte, ist bekannt. Siegel's Division wurde dem Feinde, der nun Zeit genug gehabt, sich gemächlich zurückzuziehn, allein entgegengeschickt, und unterdessen waren plötzlich die übrigen Divisionen zum schleunigen Rückzug aufgebrochen und hatten einzig unsre deutsche Division in Springfield zurückgelassen. Auch Siegel und wir fanden schließlich unsern Weg zu den andern nach Rolla an die Eisenbahn, die uns allenfalls hätte nach St. Louis bringen können. Wir hatten letztes Spätjahr zuversichtlich gehofft, bis Weihnachten im warmen Dixieland Winter und Kälte hinter uns, den Feind vor uns zu haben; und nun lagen wir fast drei Monate lang unthätig, aber weit weg vom Feind und sicher bei Rolla auf dem Schnee. Wiederum wurde ich an Wallensteins Lager erinnert, aber diesmal an die Worte der Kapuzinerpredigt: „Und die Armee liegt hier in Böhmen, – Pflege den Bauch, läßt sich's wenig grämen, – kümmert sich mehr um den Krug als den Krieg – " oder – mußte ich unwillkürlich daran flicken – „Kümmert sich nur um Trank und Speis – Und gibt dem Price Missouri Preis." –

Man verzeihe mir diese Abschweifung! Ich habe meinen Mißmuth doch nur in die unschuldigen Zeilen meines Tagebuchs ausgehaucht; bei härtern Soldatennaturen mag er mitgeholfen haben, die Feuer zu schüren, welche von dem Mittag an, da wir einzogen, bis zum nächsten Morgen in die 20 Häuser und darunter eine Anzahl gerade der schönsten des unglücklichen

---

[58] „retirirt", verdeutschtes part. perf. von *retire* – zurückziehen.

Springfields in Asche gelegt hatten. Auch Fremonts´ ehemaliges Hauptquartier traf dies Loos, und mancher, den noch jeder Brand kalt gelassen, ergrimmte über den Sturz dieses Denkmals an eine Zeit, da unsre kriegerische Begeisterung am höchsten gelodert, aber nicht Ein Haus in Springfield zerstört hatte.

Wir waren kaum an den letzten Häusern Springfields vorüber, als auf einer gegenüberliegenden Höhe, getrennt durch einen Bach, eine Menge Barracken sichtbar wurden. Sie wurden uns als Lager angewiesen, und neugierig machten wir uns darüber her, zu sehn, was für Winterquartiere sich unre Feinde hergerichtet hätten. Es schien dies das Hauptlager gewesen zu sein, und doch konnten hier nicht viel mehr als 3 Regimenter Platz gehabt haben. Der Gruppierung nach hatten jedenfalls verschiedene Truppenabtheilungen hier gelegen. Nur wenige kleine runde Zelte mussten, den zurückgelassenen Spuhren zufolge, hier und wieder zwischen den Baraken gestanden haben. Diese selber waren wesentlich verschieden von denjenigen, welche ein Theil unsrer Truppen sich bei Rolla gebaut hatte. Unsre Barraken stellten lange Gebäude, halb Block – halb Frainhäuser vor, so geräumig, daß gut ein halbes Battalion in einem Platz fand; 3 über einander befestigte, breite Bettstellen, der Mangel an Licht und Matrazen

Ende der 10. Manuskriptseite

gaben ihnen große Aehnlichkeit mit dem Zwischendeck eines Auswandererschiffes sowie einen fruchtbaren Boden für Ungeziefer; auch der Gesundheitszustand sprach keineswegs zu ihren Gunsten. Im Gegensatz dazu waren diese feindlichen Barraken kleine niedrige Blockhäuser, mit Lehm beworfen und ausgekittet, gut gesichert gegen Wind und Kälte. Entweder waren es längere Gebäude, die durch Wände in vollständig abgesonderte Räume getheilt waren, oder frei stehende kleine Häuschen; alle aber waren sie ausgezeichnet durch hübsche, aus Backsteinen erbaute Kamine, überhaupt so wohnlich eingerichtet wie möglich. Kein Wunder, daß unsre Jungens große Augen dazu machten und davon Veranlassung nahmen zu raisonieren, denn raisonieren muß d. Soldat und desto mehr, je besser er es hat.

In dem Nebengebäude eines ehemaligen Farmhauses, welcher eine Aufschrift als das bisherige Quartier des Commissärs bezeichnete, fanden wir zu unserer nicht geringen Freude, noch etwas Vorräthe von Kornmehl, frischen Schinken und gedörrte Apfelschnitze, gerade genug, daß wir diesen und den nächsten Tag zu leben hatten. Das heißt denn doch: feurige Kohlen aufs Haupt des Feindes sammeln, wir verbrennen den Sezessionisten die Häuser, und sie geben uns Obdach und Speise. Wahrlich, dieser Price muß ein humaner, charmanter Mann sein oder – sehr große Eile gehabt haben. Ohne seine Fürsorge hätten wir bei einer eisigen Kälte, die sich von Stunde zu Stunde steigerte, ohne Nahrung den Rest des Tages und die Nacht wiederum auf der freien Erde zubringen müssen. Denn nur wenige von unsern Wagen erreichten uns an diesem Tage, und diese brachten die Tornister nach und hatten wieder umzukehren, um die unterwegs abgeladenen, d. i. abgeworfenen Waaren nachzuholen, mit Ausnahme dessen, was die Fuhrleute unter dem Commando eines sorgsamen Quartiermeisters zertrümmert hatten oder and der Straße liegen zu lassen beliebten.

Noch habe ich einer Hinterlassenschaft des Feindes zu erwähnen, einiger schwer Kranken, die unter der Sorge eines Arztes in einer der Barraken zurückgeblieben waren. Auch an ihnen war keine Spuhr von Uniform oder dergleichen zu entdecken, überhaupt war da keine Spuhr von Comfort. Der Arzt, ein jüngerer Mann, fast kindlich offen und unschuldig in seinem Aeußern wie in seinen Reden und stolz darauf, daß er seine Kranken nicht im Stiche ließe, erzählte uns, daß seine Armee in d letzten Nacht aufgebrochen wäre, daß sie 10 – 12,000 Mann zähle und ausschließlich aus Missouriern bestünde, mit Ausnahme der Artillerie, welche ihre Hauptstärke ausmachte, daß Price in der hiesigen Gegend sich nicht stellen würde, und er dies auch letes Spätjahr nicht beabsichtigt hätte, sondern sich so weit zurückziehn werde, bis er auf

Ende der 11. Manuskriptseite

dem Boden von Arkansas Verstärkung durch südlich Truppen erhielt, die ihm in bedeutender Zahl angesagt wäre. Auf die Frage, ob sie auch schon Sold bezogen hätten – ein sehr wesentlicher Punkt! – erwiederte er, daß die Ärzte bei ihnen überhaupt nicht bezahlt würden. Übrigens schien er nur noch geringe Hoffnung in das Gelingen der Revolution zu setzen und es sogar zu bedauern, sich derselben angeschlossen zu haben. Er richtete diese Erzählung an einen unsrer Aerzte, mit dem er weiland auf einen der medicin. Collegien in St. Louis studiert hatte und hier zum ersten Mal nach Jahren wieder zusammen traf.

Es läßt sich denken daß unsre Freude nicht gar groß war, als wir nächsten Morgen unsre warmen Barraken verlassen mußten, um dem Feinde nachzujagen, während unsre Wagen mit Zelten und Proviant uns noch nicht eingeholt hatten und zur Beschleunigung des Marsches auch noch die Tornister zurückgelassen w. mußten. Es herrschte eine frostige Kälte; ein scharfer Wind blies uns ins Gesicht, der Boden war m. Glatteis bedeckt und unsre Bärte mit Eiszapfen behangen. Doch trösteten wir uns damit, dem Feinde in Wilson's Creek, wie es hieß, daß er eine feste Stellung eingenommen hätte, zu begegnen und dort die alte Scharte auszuwetzen. Auch ermunterte sich mancher mit d. schlechten Troste, daß für die feindliche Armee die Kälte ungewohnter und darum doppelt empfindl. und nachtheilig sei. Die waren doppelt betrogen; der Feind bestund ja fast ausschließl. aus Missouriern, die dies Clima nicht minder gewohnt waren wie wir, u. an e. Schlacht dachte er gar nicht.

Wir waren etwa 2 Meilen weit gegangen, als wir auf e. weiten Felde die erste Division in Schlachtlinie aufgestellt fanden; auch den unsrigen wurde ihr Platz als Reserve angewiesen. Die verschiedenen Corps nahmen ihre Stellung ein; Generäle und Adjutanten sprengten daher, und Alles sah sich begierig nach d. Feinde um. Da, vor uns auf einem Hügel gewahrten wir eine lange dunkle Reihe, vor einem Gehölze aufgepflanzt; unsre Herrn Stabsofficiere griffen nach ihren Opernguckern und entdeckten, daß es – Fenceriegel waren.

Nach einer Weile geriethen die Reihen der vor uns stehenden Division in wirre Bewegung; wir sahen Colonnen im Doppelquick herumspringen, und vermochten doch nicht, ein ordentl. Jägermanöver herauszulesen. Bald stellten auch unsre Soldaten ihre Gewehre in Pyramiden zusammen und begannen nach dem Beispiel von uns, herumzutanzen und sich zu boxen. Es war aber weder die Tanz-, noch die Prügelwuth, denen ja auch nachgesagt wird, daß sie ansteckend wären, sondern einfach die grimmige Kälte, die uns in dieser kalten Zeitalter trieb, erst die Possen des Mittelalters nachzuahmen, dann aber über eine nahe Fence herzufallen und Feuer anzumachen.

Dem Stande der Sonne nach – denn unsre Uhren waren längst stehen geblieben – ging es auf Mittag zu,

Ende der 12. Manuskriptseite

als sich die Schlachtlinie wieder auflöste und der Zug, wie gewohnt, in Bewegung setzte. Leider bin ich kein Stratege und so konnte ich mir auch nicht erklären, warum wir in Schlachtordnung gestellt worden waren gegen einen Feind, der sich bis heute nocht nicht hat blicken lassen. Ein Capitain, den die Kälte gleich ungeduldig gestimmt haben mochte, wandte sich an einen unsrer Stabsofficiere mit der Frage, warum wir nicht vorrückten, nachdem wir uns vollständig zum Angriff aufgestellt hatten, und erhielt drüber folgenden Aufschluß: Price ist noch nicht bereit; wir müßen erst warten, bis er seine Schlachtlinie geordnet hat. Es mochte etwas wahres daran sein, daß wir erst warten mußten, bis es Price gefällig wäre, sich mit uns einzulassen. Ich notiere dies aber weniger zur Erklärung unsres Maneuvres als zur Charakterisierung mancher Officiere in unsern Freiwilligen Regimentern; denn unser höherer Militair, der jene Antwort gab, hatte es vollständig ernst gemeint, und mit demselben Ernste theilte es der Capitain seiner Companie mit.

Ein Weg von 10 Meilen, wobei wir das ehemalige Schlachtfeld von Wilson's Creek weit links südlich liegen ließen, brachte uns nach Little York, einem kleinen Städtchen, was damals aus wenig mehr als 2 kurzen Häuserreihn zu beiden Seiten der Straße bestand. Wie viel jetzt noch davon steht, kann ich mit Bestimmtheit nicht sagen; als wir es erreichten, stand das äußerste Haus in Flammen und, wie das Gerüchte ging, passierte der letzte Theil unsres Trains nur noch rauchende Trümmer.

Hier hatten abends zuvor ein paar Companien unsrer unermüdlichen deutschen Cavallerie das Ende des feindl. Trains aufgejagt und eine bedeutende Zahl Wagen weggenommen und von da nach Springfield zurückgebracht. Als Opfer des dabei stattgefundenen Scharmützels fanden wir noch die Leichen einiger Sezessionisten im Gehölze unmittelbar an der Straße und in einem benachbarten Hause einen Verwundeten, einen Jungen von kaum 18 Jahren, der sich noch recht leidlich befand, trotzdem eine Kugel durch seine rechte Brust dicht neben dem Brustbein hinein – und neben dem Rückrath hinausgegangen war.

Ein paar Meilen außerhalb Little Yorks wurde auf einer weiten, steinigen Prairie Halt gemacht und den verschiedenen Truppenabtheilungen ihr Lagerplatz für die kommende Nacht angewiesen. Ein unfreundlicheres Lager hatten wir noch nie gehabt. Ein zerfallenes kleines Blockhaus wurde zum Hauptquartier gemacht, darin der General mit s. Stab residierte. Dicht daran, in einem spärlichen niedern Gehölze, wenn es diesen Namen verdient, suchten unsre Truppen Schutz vor dem scharfen Winde. Die Kälte, welche durch die Mittagssonne etwas gemildert worden war, erreichte wieder die frühere eisige Höhe. Nur <u>ein</u> Wagen mit ein paar Zelten hatte uns eingeholt. Holy für Feuer war, wie angedeutet, spärlich, und die Lebensmittel bestanden hauptsächlich aus einigen Schafen, Kälbern und Gänsen, die uns bei Little York in den Weg gekommen und als Kriegsgefangene mitgeschleppt worden waren.

Zu den Glücklichsten gehörte ich. Und unsre Glieder, bei dem Mangel an Zelten und Decken nicht allzusehr dem Froste und dem epidemisch gewordenen Rheumatismus preiszugeben, sucht ich mit 2 andern Officieren in einem kleinen Frainhaus, 1 ½ Meilen vom Regiment entfernt und nahe unsern Vor posten, ein Obdach. Haus und Stallungen standen leer; eine

Ende der 13. Manuskriptseite

alte wurmstichige Bettstätte war das einzige, was die Besitzer zurückgelassen, und sie zu Stücken zerschlagen und daraus ein mächtiges Feuer im Kamin anzumachen, unser erstes Geschäft. Das zweite bestund darin, die Fenster mit ihren zerbrochenen Scheiben mit Brettern zu vernageln, um uns vor dem scharfen Durchzug zu sichern. Dann zerstreuten sich unsre Bursche nach allen Seiten, um aufzutreiben, was unter solchen Umständen dienlich sein mochte. Futter für unsre Pferde und Stroh für die Nachtlager war das Erste und Nothwendigste was sie herbeischleppten. Ein Sack mit Backweizenmehl und ein Topf voll Schmalz, die in einem benachbarten Gebäude aufgefunden wurden, kamen sehr erwünscht. Dagegen Wasser mußte 2 Meilen weit hergeholt werden, glich eher Kaffesatz und war, genauer definiert, weiter nichts als Koth in tropfbar-flüßiger Form. Dessenungeachtet wurde uns bei dem hellen, warmen Kaminfeuer, um welches wir auf Holzblöcke gelagert saßen, immer behaglicher zu Muthe, und mit der einbrechenden Nacht waren wir so reichlich versorgt, daß uns nichts – am wenigsten ein gesunder Appetit, zum Abendessen und überhaupt zur Glückseligkeit fehlte. Denn eine Kaffekanne, eine Pfanne, ein Säckchen voll Kaffe und ein anderes mit Zucker führten unsre Burschen immer mit sich, und hinter uns schrien ein paar fette Gänse, die unterwegs aufgefangen worden und sich mit zusammengebundenen Füßen auf dem Fußboden herumwälzten. So steckten wir denn unsre Pfeifen an und begannen um die Wette, aus den vorhandenen Naturalien ein möglichst civilisiertes Mahl zu bereiten. Einer enthauptete die Gefangenen; zwei balgten sie aus, da zum Rupfen weder Licht noch Geduld genug vorhanden war; ein vierter ließ Gänsefett aus und rührte aus dem gefundenen Mehl und dem sogenannten Wasser den Teig zu einer Art Pfannkuchen zurecht; ein fünfter endlich schüttete einen Haufen Kaffe – geröstet, wie er von der Regierung geliefert wird – in einen schmutzigen Brodsack, das appetitlichste Stück Zeug, das an uns zu finden, und klopfte ihn mit e. Stück Holz so lange, bis er „gemahlen" war. Gesättigt und ermüdet, legten wir uns spät erst auf's Stroh, um bald tief einzuschlafen und mit dem Erlöschen des Feuers und dem Eintreten eines empfindlichen Morgenfrostes steif zu frieren.

(ENDMARKIERUNG)

Ein Feldzug von Missouri und Arkansas.
Bilder aus dem amerikanischen Kriegsleben.
Von einem ehemaligen Offizier des 15. Missouri-Infanterie (Schweizer) Regiments.[59]

I.

Vorangegangene Ereignisse. Die Südwest-Armee. Der Marschbefehl und seine nächsten Folgen

Der Sommer 1861, der erste des Bürgerkrieges, fiel für die Unionstruppen in Missouri ungünstig aus. In kleineren Abtheilungen durchs Land zerstreut, fanden sie überall den Feind in Übermacht sich gegenüber und wurden zum Rückzuge oder zur Übergabe gezwungen. Ihre größte Armee unter General Lyons wurde in der Schlacht bei Wilson's Creek in der Nähe von Springfield aufs Haupt geschlagen; Lyons selbst fiel, seine Truppen zogen sich hastig auf St. Louis zurück. Fast alles Land südlich vom Missourifluß war jetzt in den Händen der Rebellen, und selbst Nord-Missouri war ihren Einfällen ausgesetzt. Die Rebellen-Armee bestand zum größten Theil aus Missouriern und wurde gelegentlich durch Truppen aus südlicheren Staaten verstärkt; ihr Anführer war der alte Price (spr.: „Preis") ein schlauer, unermüdlicher General und ein äußerst populärer, durch ihre äußere Erscheinung sowohl als durch geistige Begabung und Beredsamkeit eine gewinnende Persönlichkeit. Der Oberbefehlshaber der Bundestruppen im Westen, Generalmajor Fremont, war mittlerweile bemüht, aus den ihm von westlichen Staaten zugesandten und in Missouri selbst rekrutirten Truppen eine Armee zu organisiren und führte endlich Ende September seine gesamten Streitkräfte ins Feld; wobey die einzelnen Armeekorps

Ende der 1. Manuskriptseite

von verschiedenen Punkten am Missouri Fluß aus in südwestlicher Richtung vordrangen und sich bey Springfield, der Hauptstadt von Südwest-Missouri vereinigten. Von hier aus wollte Fremont dem Feinde, welcher bisher überall vor uns zurückgewichen war und sich gleichfalls concentriert hatte, mit seiner gesamt Armee nachrüken und hin zwischen hier und der Grenze von Arkansas zu einer entscheidenden Schlacht zu nöthigen. Da wurde er durch einen Befehl von Washington des Comandos enthoben und sein Nachfolger gab sofort den Befehl zum Rückzug. Ein Theil der Armee wurde nach einem anderen Kriegsschauplatz geschickt; der Rest, darunter auch unsere Division, bezog Winterquartiere halbwegs zwischen Springfield und St. Louis bey Rolla, der letzten Station einer nach St. Louis führenden Eisenbahn, und

---

[59] Der Untertitel "Bilder aus dem amerikanischen Kriegsleben" wurde scheinbar nachträglich mit Rotstift eingefügt.

bildete fortan die "Armee des Südwestens". Der Feind war uns natürlich auf dem Fuße gefolgt und zerstreute sich über das von uns aufgegebene Land; Price selber schlug in Springfield sein Hauptquartier auf. Die Süd-West Armee aber lag zwey und einen halben Monat lang, von Mitte November bis Ende Januar, theils in Baracken, theils unter Zelten, bey Rolla auf dem Schnee und auf der faulen Haut – kümmerte sich mehr um den Krug als den Krieg – wetzte lieber den Schnabel als den Sabel – dachte nur an Trank und Speis und gab dem Price Missouri preis.

Anfang Januar wurde zum Oberfehlshaber der Südwestarmee der Brigade- General Curtis ernannt, ein früherer Advokat oder Politiker, mit dem en bon point und der leuchtend rothen Gesichts-, besonders Nasenfarbe und dem etwas jovialen Ausdruck des ächten Landadvokaten und Friedensrichters im „Großen Westen", ein Mann von Vermögen, Familie und Einfluß, und, wie sich später zeigte, als er Militärgouverneur von Arkansas und dessen Baumwolle war, ein ebenso glücklicher wie geschickter Geschäftsmann. Der neue General

Ende der 2. Manuskriptseite

begrüßte seine Armee mit einem Tagesbefehl, worin er verkündigte, es stünde ein mühsamer Feldzug durch ein rauhes, unwirthsames Gebirgsland bevor, und befahl, sich darauf vorzubereiten und alles irgendwie Entbehrliche sich vom Halse zu schaffen. Was für ein Gebirgsland hier gemeint war, konnten wir leicht errathen; wir kannten es nur zu gut von unserem Rückzuge von Springfield her und erinnerten uns jetzt wieder lebhaft und mit Grausen an jene wilde Gegend, welche noch immer so aussieht, als ob nur Indianer und Hasen dort hausten, und an die rauhen, steilen Gebirgswege und die unsägliche Thierquälerey, welche unsere armen Maulesel zu erleiden hatten und der so mancher von ihnen zum Opfer gefallen war.

Der Endruck, welchen dieser Aufruf des obersten Kriegsherrn unter seinen Heerscharen hervorrief, bestund darin, daß eine Menge unserer Krieger, darunter auch Offiziere auch der eine oder andere, erlaubt oder unerlaubter Weise sich zu drücken suchten. Hunderte von Soldaten drängten sich zu ihren Ärzten, um wegen chronischer Krankheiten oder unheilbarer Leibschäden in den Spitälern zurückgelassen oder vom Dienste verabschiedet zu werden – fast alles Gebrechen, welche oft schon viele Jahre alt, ihre Inhaber nicht im mindesten gehindert hatten, in den Dienst zu treten und darin zu verbleiben, solange ohne große Strapatzen und Gefahren auf Staatskosten gelebt und Sold bezogen wurde, deren sie sich aber auf einmahl lebhaft erinnerten, als der mühsame Feldzug angekündigt wurde. Es war auch in der That unglaublich, welche Schäden und wie viele derer in unseren Regimentern jetzt an den Tag kamen, Altersschwäche und theilweise Erblindung, fehlen von Fingern an der rechten Hand und verkrüppelte Füße, Schwindsucht und Herzfehler, alte Fußgeschwüre und Brüche von jeder Sorte und Länge – kurz, eine reichhaltige Sammlung von Prachtexemplaren aller derjenigen Gebrechen, welche die Armee Regulations ausdrücklich und namentlich als solche bezeichnen, welche den Eintritt in die Armee verbieten.

Ende der 3. Manuskriptseite

Natürlich wurden solche Leute als unbrauchbar verabschiedet, aber die Folge zeigte, dass eine gute Zahl derselben sich später wieder anwerben ließ, um ein gutes Handgeld zu erhalten und sich nach kurzer Zeit von neuem wegen körperlicher Untauglichkeit verabschieden zu lassen. Es gab genug Werber, welche diesen Betrug ausführen und die vorgeschriebene ärztliche Untersuchung umgehen halfen; ihnen war nur daran gelegen, eine Anzahl Rekruten herbeizuschaffen, um darauf ihre Ansprüche auf ein Offizierspatent zu gründen. Und es gelang; zerlumpte Wirthe und Bierkellner, Schuhflicker und Flickschneider wurden so Lieutenants und Kapitains. Mancher half mit dem guten Solde dieser Stellen seinen zerrütteten Finanzen wieder auf; mancher machte sogar sein Glück; jeder aber fand seine Rechnung dabey. Der Schneider verhalf dem Krüppel zum Handgeld und der Krüppel verhalf dem Schneider zur Offiziersgage. „Eine Hand wäscht die andere" – gilt als Grundsatz im Geschäftsleben, und das Soldatseyn war eben auch ein Geschäft.

II.
Der Aufbruch. Wagen und Wege. Die verlorene Regimentsmusik.

Unsere Südwest-Armee zählte beym Abmarsch, nachdem ihre Reihen auf die angegebene Weise gelichtet worden waren, noch ca. 12,000[60] Mann combatanten; war mit allem Nöthigen reichlich ausgerüstet und vortrefflich bewaffnet und bestand aus Fußvolk, Reiterei und schwerem Geschütz von verschiedenem Kaliber, von 24pfündern bis zu leichten, von Mauleseln getragenen Bergkanonen. Diese Truppen waren in vier Divisionen vertheilt; die erste Division unter Oberst Osterhaus und die zweite, zu welcher unser Regiment gehörte, unter Brigade-General Asboth, einem Ungarn, beyde zum weitaus größten Theil aus Deutschen bestehend,

Ende der 4. Manuskriptseite

bildeten das Commando des Brigade Generals Sigel. Die dritte und vierte Division fast ausschließlich Amerikaner, stunden unter dem Befehl der Obersten Davis und Carr. – Diese Divisionen brachen gegen Ende Januar einzeln und zu verschiedener Zeit auf und traten ihren Marsch auf zwei fast parallelen Straßen an. Unsere Division war die letzte, welche Marschbefehl erhielt; dennoch dauerte es acht volle Tage, bis derselbe befolgt wurde, d. h. bis wir die nöthige Zahl von Wagen und Maulthieren hatten, um unser Gepäck, Proviant und Munition fortzuschaffen. Denn damals war es noch nicht wie zwei Jahre später unter Sherman u. a., dass der Soldat einen Theil

---

[60] In der wörtlich abgeschriebenen Fassung wird „12-14,000" angeführt.

der kleinen Zelte samt Kochgeschirr auf seinem Tornister und der Offizier sein Gepäck in einer Tasche zu tragen hatte. Wir lebten in der guten Zeit, wo noch die alten Armee-Regulationen in Kraft waren, wie sie vor dem Kriege für die reguläre Armee und ihre weiten Märsche auf den Prairien des Westens gegolten hatten. Jede Compagnie hatte einen Wagen, welcher ihre großen Zelte, Munition, Kochgeschirr und anderes Compagnieeigenthum trug, sowie das Gepäck ihrer Offiziere, große Koffern, Feldbetten, selbst Öfen. Außerdem hatten die Stabsoffiziere einen Wagen, die Ärzte einen, welcher das Nöthigste zur Herrichtung eines Feldspitals trug, und der Quartiermeister ein paar Wägen. Jeder dieser schweren Frachtwagen war mit vier Mauleseln bespannt – starke, prächtige Thiere von der Größe eines mittelgroßen Pferdes. Daraus mag man berechnen, welch ein Troß von Roß und Zeisigen jedem Regimente folgte, und wie schwerfällig die Bewegungen einer solchen Colonne seyn mußten; zumal wenn man die schlechte Beschaffenheit amerikanischer Straßen in Betracht zieht.

Ende der 5. Manuskriptseite

Viel leichter und schneller als mit dem Fortschaffen des Nothwendigen ging es mit dem Zurücklassen des Entbehrlichen. Alles, was nicht Privat-Eigenthum war, Zelte, Öfen u.s.f. wurde einfach liegen gelassen, wo es gerade lag, in der Voraussicht, der Chef des Quartiermeisterdepots zu Rolla (es war dies der damalige Hauptmann Sheridan, der nachmals so berühmte General) werde darnach sehen und es abholen lassen. Wenn dies nicht so bald geschah und mittlerweile zurückgebliebene Soldaten und andere gefällige Nachbarn vom Civilstand sich beflissen, das Fortschaffen zu erleichtern, so thaten sie damit unentgeldlich nur dasselbe, was tausende, welche besoldet waren, mit dem Staatseigenthum auch thaten.

Es war am Vormittag des 1ten Februars 1862, als unser Regiment endlich abmarschierte. Voran schritt die hübsche Musikbande mit den theilweis silbernen Instrumenten, dann kam das Regiment mit seinen vielen Offizieren, im Ganzen kaum mehr als 600 Mann; unmittelbar dahinter zwey Ambulancewagen, von denen einer die ersten Gefallenen nachführte, zwey schwerbetrunkene Offiziere, einen Hauptmann, Müller von Profession, und einen Lieutenant, einem ehemaligen Barbier. Als Schluß folgte unter dem Knallen der Peitschen und den Flüchen der Fuhrleute—alle Soldaten des Regiments, welche dazu detachiert waren—die lange Reihe der hochbeladenen Wagen, und auf diesen hin und wieder Offiziers-Burschen, kleine Jungen mit aufblühenden Spitzbuben-Gesichtern, welche hier die Schule des Lebens genoßen; sonst wiegten sich wohl auch auf der Höhe der Wagen Wäscherinnen und anderes weibliches Gesinde von beliebiger Farbe, weiß, gelb oder schwarz; diesmahl aber

Ende der 6. Manuskriptseite

war dergleichen Baggage als irgendwie entbehrlich zurückgelassen worden.

Während der lezten 8 Tage hatte der Himmel mit Regen, Schnee und Frost sein Möglichstes gethan, um uns von dem bevorstehenden Marsche das Schlimmste befürchten zu lassen; und wirklich rechtfertigte gleich der erste Tag diese Befürchtungen vollkommen. Kaum 100 Schritte außerhalb des Bereichs der ehemaligen Lagerplätze, welche wir jetzt durchzogen, blieb unser erster Wagen im Moraste stecken, und in nächster Nähe davon wurde unser ganzer Train zum Stehen gebracht, indem ein Munitionswagen der Artillerie so tief eingesunken war, daß 10 Pferde sich vergeblich anstrengten, denselben vom Fleck zu schaffen.

Noch tiefer als der Eindruck, den dieser Wagen in den Weg gemacht, mußte der Eindruck seyn, den der Weg auf unsere Musikanten machte; denn so sehr diese, wie alle Musikanten, große Freunde vom Naß waren, so jagte ihnen diesmahl das Naß ihrer Füße und der ganze schöne Anfang zu dem verheißenen, mühsamen Feldzuge einen derartigen Schreck ein, daß Einer nach dem Andern von ihnen zurückblieb; und als Abends Appel gehalten wurde, stellte es sich heraus, daß die ganze Musikbande mit ihren silbernen und blechernen[61] Instrumenten mit Sack und Pack sich in corpore aus dem Staub gemacht hatte. - Als nach einiger Zeit wieder Zeitungen aus St. Louis uns zu Gesichte kamen, lasen wir darin eine Einladung an das geehrte Publikum zu der musikalischen Abendunterhaltungen kamen, lasen wir darin eine Einladung an das geehrte Publikum zu den musikalischen Abendunterhaltungen der rühmlich bekannten Regimentsmusik des "Schweizer-Regiments". Für uns war diese Bande auf immer verloren, und wir begnügten uns fortan mit unseren Tambouren und Trompetern. Erstere, Jungens von 15 - 17 Jahren, welche große hölzerne Trommeln recht wacker bearbeiteten, Leztere junge Männer, welche sich alle Mühe gaben, auf in einem einzigen Bogen gewundenen Blechröhren

Ende der 7. Manuskriptseite

die Ohrenzerreißensten Mißtöne hervorzubringen. Manche amerikanischen Regimenter hatten statt dieser sog. Trompeter die altehrwürdigen Pfeifer, und wenn diese im Chor mit den Holztrommeln einen amerikanischen oder Irrländischen (im anderen Manuskript: irländischen) Nationalmarsch anhuben, so klang es gerade wie die Musik zu einem Bärentanz.

III.
Militärischer Gehorsam. Der erste Bivouac. Ein Missouri-Blockhaus.
Rüstig zogen wir vorwärts durch den Schnee über das buschige Hügelland. Das Ziel unseres heutigen Marsches sollte die Stelle seyn, wo das Flüßchen Little Piney in den Gebirgsstrom Gasconade mündet. Als wir aber noch 4 1/2 Meilen (d. i. 1 1/2 Stunden) davon entfernt waren, erklärten einige Offiziere, nicht mehr weiter gehen zu wollen, bevor uns die Wagen mit Zelten und

---

[61] In der Abschrift steht „messingenen" anstatt „blechernen".

Proviant eingeholt hätten. Der Oberst gab den Befehl zum Weitermarsch, aber umsonst! Die Zahl der widerspenstigen Offiziere mehrte sich, ihre Forderung, hier Halt zu machen, wurde peremptorischer; und so blieb dem Oberst nur die Wahl, entweder mit einer kleinen Zahl Getreuer weiter zu marschieren oder aber gut demokratisch sich dem Willen der Mehrheit zu fügen und damit gegen den ihm vom General gegebenen Befehl ungehorsam zu seyn, nachdem ihm selber von seinen Untergebenen der Gehorsam gekündigt worden war.

Der gute Oberst gab nach, und wir machten Halt, um auf unseren Train zu warten. Doch derselbe erschien nicht, und so waren wir genöthigt, auf dem Felde einer am Wege liegenden Farm zu bivouakiren. Auf dem Schnee einem äußerst frostigen Winde ausgesetzt, dabey ohne etwas Warmes im Leib zu haben, verbrachten wir diese erste Nacht. Einer kleinen Anzahl von uns war es vergönnt, in einem der zwey Blockhäuser Obdach und Speise zu finden. Der Farmer war ein Unionsmann, ein echter Missourischer Unionsmann, wie wir sie zur Genüge hatten kennenlernen, äußerst kurz
Ende der 8. Manuskriptseite

in seinen Reden, ohne jede Neigung, sich nach amerikanischem Brauche in ein Gespräch über Politik oder Krieg einlassen zu wollen, und offenbar sehr unzufrieden mit unserem Besuche; für seinen Kaffee und Speck ließ er sich reichlich bezahlen, sogar für die Erlaubniß, auf dem Boden seiner Hütte schlafen zu dürfen, 1/4 Dollar die Person, und war äußerst entrüstet, als seine unverschämte Rechnung für verbrannte Fenceriegel (Zaunpflöcke#) und einige geschossene Spahnferkel vom Oberst ganz bedeutend reduziert wurde. Auch sein Blockhaus war das Original der Behausung eines kleinen Missourischen Farmers, ein einfacher Raum mit zwey sich gegenüber stehenden Thüren ohne Schlösser und Riegel, dagegen mit einer Lücke im rohen Holz, durch welche die Hand hinausgestreckt wurde, um die fest anliegende massive Thüre aufzureißen, natürlich auch ohne Fenster, dagegen voller Lücken und Löcher an Dach und Wänden—ein Moskitonetz, wie einer unserer Offiziere es nannte, welcher nicht Worte genug finden konnte, um seine Entrüstung auszudrücken über eine derartige Nachlässigkeit und Faulheit eines alten Ansiedlers mit 160 Juchardt guten Landes und ein paar erwachsenen Söhnen. Noch schlimmer sah übrigens das dahinterstehende kleinere Blockhaus drein, worin der eine Sohn mit seiner hübschen jungen Frau und verschiedenen Sprößlingen hauste.

Auf dem Fußboden dieser Hütten lagen ohne weitere Unterlage oder Decke als den Überrock unsere meisten Offiziere im Halbkreis ausgestreckt, die Füße dem Kamin

---

#in Amerika ist jedes Stück angebauten Landes von einem Zaune („Fence") umgeben, welcher aus kürzeren und längeren Pflöcken („Fenceriegel") besteht.

Ende der 9. Manuskriptseite

zugekehrt, welcher aus Steinen aufgethürmt, einem ans Haus hingebauten Festungsthurme voller Schiesscharten glich und so umfänglich war, daß ein wahrer Scheiterhaufen von gewaltigen Stücken halber und ganzer Baumstämme darin loderte, deren Hitze Einigen die Stiefel verbrannte, während ihr entfernter liegender Oberkörper aufs Empfindlichste fror.

Den folgenden Morgen erschien unser Quartiermeister mit der erfreulichen Nachricht, daß unsere Fuhrwerke noch immer nicht vom Flecke kämen. So mußten wir also nach der durchfrorenen Nacht auch noch eines erwärmenden Kaffees und überhaupt der Speise entsagen, einige Schweinchen abgerechnet, die geschossen und gebradten wurden. Zur Erhöhung der Annehmlichkeit unseres Lagers erhob sich ein tüchtiges Schneegestöber, welches den ganzen Tag und bis in die Nacht hinein anhielt.

Endlich zwischen 2 und 3 Uhr trafen unsere Wagen ein; aber schon vorher war auch unser General zurückgeritten gekommen, um sich nach der Ursache unseres Ausbleibens zu erkundigen und uns zu befehlen, sofort weiterzumarschieren. Es blieb uns also eben Zeit, in aller Geschwindigkeit einen Kaffee zu sieden und dann die noch fehlenden 4 1/2 Meilen zurückzulegen.

Es läßt sich denken, wie behaglich mir am Abend dieses Tages zu Muthe war, da ich endlich in einem warmen Zelte, geschützt vor dem Schneegestöber, neben einer Tasse heißen Thee mit Brantwein auf meinem Feldbette ausgestreckt lag und auf meinem Koffer unsere jüngsten Erlebnisse in mein Tagebuch eintrug, ohne eine andere Sorge zu kennen, als die, daß ich mit meinen Füßen den Boden berühren möchte, welcher, nachdem der Schnee unter der Ofenhitze geschmolzen, einen wahren Morast darstellte. Denn zu den Annehmlichkeiten des Offiziersstandes

Ende der 10. Manuskriptseite

gehörte ein kleiner Ofen, welcher hie und da Einer so glücklich war, als Zubehör zu seinem Zelte vom Quartiermeister zu beziehen, und welcher einen Cylinder von[62] Eisenblech darstellte, ohne Boden, aber mit einem Thürchen und einem langen geraden Rohre versehen, welches zur Spitze des Zeltes hinausragte.

IV.
Über Berg und Thal. Ein Landstädchen im Westen. Soldaten Logik.

Der nächste Morgen brachte uns schönes Wetter; der Boden war mit festem Schnee bedeckt, und diesem Umstande dankten wir es, daß trotz der

---

[62] Die Abschrift führt „von starkem Eisenblech" anstatt „von Eisenblech" an.

steilen Gebirgswege unsere Fuhrwerke fortan Schritt mit uns hielten. Zunächst ging es 9 Meilen weit durch dünn besiedelte Thäler und über einen hohen Berg bis wir in eine tiefe, enge Schlucht hinabstiegen und auf einen wirren Knäuel von Fuhrwerken, Geschützen, Fußvolk und Reiterei stießen, welche sich alle drängten, einen vor uns liegenden kleinen Fluß, die Big-Piney, zu durchschreiten. Es war ein Theil unserer eigenen und ein Theil der ersten Division mit denen wir hier zum ersten Mahl zusamentrafen. Die Menschenmasse war aber keineswegs so groß, als die Zahl der hier vertretenen Truppenkörper hätte vermuthen lassen. Es waren nicht mehr die vollzähligen 900–1000 Mann starken Regimenter, welche leztes Spätjahr unter der Führung Freemonts mit uns in Feld gezogen waren. Witterung, Strapatzen und vor allem die hier zu Lande herrschenden Gallenfieber und Typhen hatten ihre Reihen gewaltig gelüftet, noch ehe ihnen der Feind zu Gesicht gekommen war. Ein einziges, ohnehin nicht starkes Illinois-Regiment hatte während der 2 1/2 Monate, die wir bey Rolla lagen, gegen 170 Mann in der fremden Erde begraben. Während derselben Zeit

Ende der 11. Manuskriptseite

waren in unserer deutschen Division nur 2 Todesfälle pro Regiment zu beklagen. Wir hatten hier Gelegenheit, an uns selber zu erfahren, wie wohltätig es für Truppen ist, zerstreut Luft und Kälte ausgesetzt in Zelten zu wohnen, wie die Leute sich dabey eines fast übermenschlichen Appetits erfreuen und stark und dick werden, und wir hatten Gelegenheit an anderen zu sehen, wie viel nachtheiliger für den Gesundheitszustand das Zusammenwohnen in großen Barraken, welche so leicht zum Heerde von Epidemien werden, (ist).

Die Big Pinney ist weder tief noch sehr reißend. Das Fußvolk wurde leicht auf den abgeladenen Bagagewagen hinübergeführt. Die Kanonen aber, besonders die zum Umwerfen bepakten Wagen machten dem geplagten Vieh oft lange und gewaltige Mühe, bis sie durch das eiskalte Wasser durchgeschleppt waren, und so nahm dieser Flußübergang den ganzen Rest des Tages in Anspruch.

Am jenseitigen Ufer der Big-Biney dehnte sich ein weiter Thalgrund aus, begrenzt von hohen waldigen Bergrücken. Als wir den nächsten Morgen die jähe Abdachung dieser Bergkette erstiegen hatten, standen wir auf der Höhe eines wilden Waldgebirges, welches sich, so weit das Auge reichte, zu beyden Seiten vor uns ausdehnte. Der fast gänzliche Mangel menschlicher Wohnungen und angebauten Landes, die Wälder und Matten, die tiefen Schluchten und die seichten Thalgründe, welche wieder in eben so hohen waldigen Bergrücken ausliefen, gaben der Gegend das Ansehen, als ob hier noch immer ein Indianerstamm seine Jagdgründe hätte. Erst spät am Nachmittag führte uns die Straße wieder bergab, und wir betraten einen tiefen Thalkessel. Hier lag das Städchen Waynesville, der Haupt Ort des Bezirks, und der Typus eines Landstädchens des amerikanischen Westens.

Den Mittelpunkt bildete das Rathhaus, das einzige steinerne Gebäude des Ortes, umgeben von einem

Ende der 12. Manuskriptseite

weiten freyen Platze, welcher anzudeuten schien, für wieviel Häuser hier noch Raum wäre, um Waynsville zu einer Stadt zu machen. In weitem Kreiß zerstreut stunden etwa 3 mittelmäßige „Frain-Häuser" d. h. ein- oder zweystöckige hölzerne Häuser, deren Wände und Dielen übergipste und deren Außenseite weiß angestrichen ist, und ein gutes Duzend Bretterbuden („Shanties") und Blockhäuser. Eine Kirche konnte ich nicht entdecken, und das zu meinem größten Erstaunen, da ich in einem Amerikanischen Flecken von zwey Duzend Häusern mindestens 3 Kirchen und doppelt so viele religiöse Gemeindschaften, erwartet hätte. Dagegen gab es eine kleine Anzahl von Straßen, freylich fast ganz ohne Häuser, alle parallel, in zwey Reihen, welche sich in rechten Winkeln kreuzten; vielleicht trugen diese Straßen auch schon Namen; gewiß aber waren die von ihnen begrenzten Vierecke schon längst sorgfältig in kleine Bauplätze abgetheilt; und diese einzeln im Besitz einer größeren Anzahl von Leuten und der Besitz urkundlich verbrieft und in der Meinung der Eigenthümer eine Geldquelle für künftige Zeiten, wenn dereinst Waynsville eine große Stadt seyn wird. Dies ist nemlich der Gang, wie hier zu Lande Städte gegründet werden, oft auf Aktien von Gesellschaften im fernen Osten. Erst werden die Straßen abgesteckt und die Bauplätze ausgelegt, dann gibt man dem Kind einen Namen, den Namen irgendeiner berühmten Person oder einer antidiluvianischen Stadt wie Memphis oder Utica, und diesen Namen läßt man von nun an auf den Landkarten verzeichnen. Und jetzt beginnt die Spekulation, die Stadt wird in den Hauptzeitungen des Landes angekündigt und angepriesen, ihre Bauplätze werden zum Verkauf angeboten, werden gekauft, in die Höhe getrieben, wieder verkauft, kurz, bilden einen Hauptgegenstand Amerikanischer

Ende der 13. Manuskriptseite

Spekulation. Mancher im Osten setzt große Hoffnungen auf solche Bauplätze in einer westlichen Stadt, welcher alles von der Zukunft erwartet, oder auf seine Ländereien im Hinterwald in Missouri oder Iowa; von Jahr zu Jahr erwartet er zu hören, daß jene Gegend plötzlich aufblühe und er damit ein reicher Grundbesitzer und Rentier werde, vorläufig aber dient sein Grundbesitz als Weide für Kühe und Gänse und bringt nur Kosten, jährliche Steuern für Stadt, Bezirk, Staat und Vereinigte Staaten. Wendet er sich ungeduldig an einen Einwohner von Wayensville oder wie immer die junge Stadt heißt, um Auskunft, so erhält er die Versicherung: die Stadt hat eine Zukunft und eine große Zukunft; sie müßte aufblühen, sobald nur erst eine Eisenbahn oder der Zug der Einwanderung dahingehe und die Gegend mehr angesiedelt sey. Von dieser Überzeugung sind alle Bewohner eines solchen Ortes durchdrungen, und alle bemühen sich, jeden Fremden, der zufällig in die Gegend kommt, festzuhalten und zur Niederlassung zu bewegen. Nur uns hielten sie nicht fest; vor uns waren fast sämtliche Einwohner von Wayenville geflohen. Die kurze Rast, welche wir in dem Städtchen machten, benützte ich dazu, das Rathhaus zu inspiciren. Alle Thüren waren aufgesperrt oder eingeschlagen, kein Mensch im unteren Stockwerk zu finden, die Archive geleert und überhaupt fast alles weggeschafft; wohl aber fand ich noch in einem der Zimmer die hohen und langen Fächer gefüllt mit jenen unvermeidlichen, in gelbes Kalbsleder gebundenen, dicken Büchern, welche die Basis eines jeden amerikanischen Gemeinwesens bilden. Es waren die Bücher, nach welchen Recht gesprochen wird, und ohne welche die Leute nicht wissen, was recht ist; und es waren ihrer so viele und sind in jedem, auch dem kleinsten Flecken der Vereinigten Staaten so viele und für jeden Staat ganz besonders, um es möglich zu machen,

Ende der 14. Manuskriptseite

daß es in Amerika mehr Advokaten gibt als in Italien Pfaffen. Mit Grauen durchflog mein Blick diese langen Reihen; dann mußte ich mich fragen: ob wohl im ganzen Bezirk so viel Blockhäuser stünden als es solcher gelber lederner Bücher bedürfen, um unter diesen Hinterwäldlern das Recht zu vertreten. Im oberen Stockwerk war ebenfalls alles leer; dagegen traf ich hier eine unerwaretete Gesellschaft, eine Gruppe Artilleristen, die hinter ihrer Batterie zurückgeblieben waren, nicht mehr wußten, wo dieselbe hingekommen, und nun beabsichtigten, sie in ruhsamer Eile gelegentlich wieder aufzusuchen. Sie ruhten sich hier aus, um ein Kaminfeuer auf dem Boden ausgestreckt und vertrieben sich die Zeit damit, daß Einer dem Andern auf hier vorgefundenen Formularen Urkunden ausstellte auf so und so viel Juchart Land im Bezirk Pulaski. – Getäuscht verließ ich das Rathhaus; meine Hausuntersuchung hatte es auf eine Karte von Missouri abgesehen, aber vergeblich! Die guten Bürger von Waynesville hatten alles irgendwie Werthvolle in Sicherheit gebracht; Nichts war zurückgeblieben als die kahlen Wände und jene ledernen Bücher, und die waren sicher.

Etwa 2 Meilen über Waynesville hinaus schlugen wir unser Lager für die kommende Nacht auf. Auf dem Wege dahin war ein Secesssionist (Sonderbündler) so unglücklich, seine Farm stehen zu haben und büßte dafür mit seinem Vorrath von Hafer, Heu, Welschkorn und Geflügel. Wie man wissen konnte, daß der Mann ein Secessionist war, daß wäre für jeden Anderen als einen Soldaten ein Räthsel gewesen; aber die Soldaten Logik schließt in allen solchen Fällen kurz und bündig: weil der Mann Etwas hat, ist er ein Secessionist; und weil er ein Secessionist ist nimmt man ihm, war er hat. Dieser Schluß ist vollkommen richtig, denn in der südlichen Armee

Ende der 15. Manuskriptseite

gilt ganz dieselbe Logik, und das Endergebniß war, daß da, wo beyde Armeen vorübergingen, keinem Menschen Etwas übrig blieb.

V.

Saubere Disciplin. Kriegsjammer

Kurz vor dem Aufbruch am nächsten Morgen spielte in unserem Regiment eine Scène, bey deren Anblick dem Offizier einer regulären Armee die Haare zu Berge gestanden wären. Der Oberst hatte einem Hauptmann irgendeinen Befehl zugeschickt und dieser kurz und grob geantwortet, er werde nicht gehorchen. Darauf reitet der Oberst zu dem Hauptmann hin und verlegt sich aufs Parlamentieren. Dieser aber stürtzt mit zornglühendem Gesicht und geballten Fäusten auf jenen los und überhäuft ihn mit einem Schwall von Flüchen, Schimpfreden und Hohngelächter, daß es kein Ende nehmen will. Dabey schreit er so laut, daß das halbe Regiment zusammenläuft, und schwingt seine Fäuste so drohend, daß alles darauf gefaßt ist, es werde sich ein Zweykampf daraus entstammen. Der Oberst aber bleibt kühl und beschränkt sich auf einen mehr geistigen (?) Widerstand, desto dichter fallen auf ihn die schwersten Schimpfwörter, welche die amerikanisch-englische Umgangssprache kennt und besonders häufig der Ausdruck Schwindler, Betrüger, Lügner - alles Worte, welche im bürgerlichen Leben unter Amerikanern im Norden einen Faustschlag, im Süden einen Revolverschuß zur unmittelbaren Folge haben würden. Alle diese Artigkeiten fließen in geläufigstem Englisch aus dem großen Maul des Hauptmanns, denn der Deutsche in Amerika bedient sich immer des Englischen, wenn er flucht; es scheint, diese Sprache eigne sich besser dazu. Das Gebahren des Hauptmanns war um so frecher, da er sich in diesem Kampfe nicht allein wußte. Es gab nemlich in unserer Freywilligen-Armee wenige Regimenter, deren

Ende der 16. Manuskriptseite

Offiziere ihren Geist nicht damit beschäftigen, Partheien zu bilden, die sich mit allen erdenklichen Intrigen bekämpften und gegenseitig aus dem Sattel zu heben suchten; regelmäßig stund an der Sptize der einen der Umsturzparthei der Oberstlieutenant, als der nächste Ihrengontesdant und der gewöhnliche Ausgang war, daß eine Anzahl Offiziere über die Klinge springen mußten, d. h. nicht etwa im Duell erlagen – Duelle waren sowohl gegen das Gesetz als gegen den Geist des Offizierscorps –, sondern einfach aus dem Dienst traten oder getreten wurden. In unserem Regiment wurde dieser Streit mit der größten Leidenschaftlichkeit und Geschäftigkeit geführt, und zwar durch wiederholte Auftritte, welche allem Anstand und jeder Disciplin Hohn sprachen. Der heutige derartige Auftritt endete damit, daß dem Hauptmann der Säbel abgenommen wurde und er künftig hinter dem Regiment her marschieren mußte, was ihm den Vortheil brachte, daß er reiten konnte. Bey nächster Gelegenheit sollte er dann vor ein Kriegsgericht gestellt werden; da es aber in der Folge an Gelegenheit oder Lust dazu gebrach und die Armeegesetze verbiethen, einen Offizier länger als eine gewisse Zeit in Untersuchungsarrest zu halten, so erhielt nach Ablauf dieser

Frist der Hauptmann Säbel und Commando zurück und war wieder der alte Offizier und Gentleman. Zwey weitere Tagemärsche führten uns durch ein Gebirgsland, niedriger und mehr angesiedelt, als der zuvor durchzogene, nach dem Städtchen Lebanon, wo wir mit der ganzen übrigen Armee zusammentrafen. Regen und Tauwetter hatten den Schnee hinweggeschmolzen, eine warme Frühlingssonne sandte ihre belebenden Strahlen auf uns herab, als Lagerplatz begrüßte uns eine anmuthige, sonnige Heide, durchflößen von einem Bach, unterbrochen von kleinen Baumgruppen und bedeckt mit hohem Grase, aus dem

Ende der 17. Manuskriptseite

unsere weißen, spitzigen Zelte wie Zauberhütten hervorragten. Hier genoßen wir ein paar Tage der angenehmsten Erholung. Es wurde gewirthschaftet, gebacken, gebraten, wie es an Sommer-Feyertagen im häuslichen Leben zu geschehen pflegt. Unsere Jungen durchstrichen mit ihren Büchsen die Gegend nach allen Richtungen; sie gingen auf die Jagd, sagten sie; aber die eigentlichen Ansiedler unserer Heide, eine schwere Menge kleiner Hasen, eine Art Kaninchen, welche bey unserer Ankunft das Weite gesucht hatten, lieferten nur eine geringe Zugabe zu unserer Tafel; die eigentliche Beute bestand in Schweinen, Schafen und Federvieh jeder Art, welche im Walde umher, wohin sie der Sicherheit wegen getrieben worden waren, oder im Gehöfe vor den Augen der Eigenthümer weggeschossen oder eingefangen wurden. Umsonst war das Weinen der Weiber, umsonst die Versicherung der Männer, daß es ihr lezter wäre und daß sie nicht wüßten, wovon sich ihre Familie ernähren, wenn ihnen auch dies noch genommen würde. Der Soldat hat kein mitleidig Herz, auch nicht für den Jammer eines so armen Volkes wie dasjenige, dem wir in Missouri begegneten, ein Volk, das mit schwerer Arbeit der Wildniß das Brod und eine Blockhütte für sein armseliges Daseyn abringt, und dessen einziger Reichthum in einem großen Kindersegen zu bestehen scheint. Sobald irgendwo ein Hase schreit oder ein Schaaf blökt, erwacht die Raubgier im Soldaten, und ist diese erst erwacht, so kennt sie keine Grenzen; er nimmt nicht nur, was er braucht, sondern auch Dinge, die für ihn keinen Nutzen haben, und was er nicht fortschleppen kann, das verfällt nur zu häufig seiner Lust zu zerstören. Noch stehen in meiner Erinnerung von unserem lezten Feldzug her die Jammergestalten zweyer Männer am Grab ihrer Habe, eines Landmannes, dessen reiche Schafheerde zerfleischt die Prairie deckte, zusammengesäbelt von einem Trupp übermüthiger Cavalleristen, und eines weinenden Schusters, dessen Schusterwerkzeuge, die einzige Quelle für den Unterhalt seiner Familie, ihm, dem deutschen Unionsmann, von einem

Ende der 18. Manuskriptseite

deutschen Soldaten schonungslos vor den Augen weggestohlen wurden. Die südlichen Truppen mochten weniger zerstören und mordbrennen als die Unsrigen, aus dem guten Grunde, weil das Land ihre Heimath war; aber um so unbarmherziger verfuhren sie mit allen denjenigen, in welchen sie Freunde des Nordens und Anhänger der rechtmäßigen Regierung erkannten. Ein langer Zug solcher Unionsleute war leztes Spätjahr der menschenfreundlichen Aufforderung Sigels gefolgt und hatte sich unter dem Schutze unserer Armee nach Rolla geflüchtet, und während unseres dortigen Aufenthaltes hatten wir Gelegenheit genug, hunderte dieser armen Flüchtlinge zu sehen, welche in der strengen Kälte des Winters von Haus und Hof vertrieben nach dieser äußersten Eisenbahnstation mit ihrem bißchen fahrender Habe geeilt kamen, um von hier aus nach dem Mississippi gebracht zu werden, und jenseits desselben im friedlichen, fruchtbaren Illinois eine neue Heimath zu gründen, während ihre alte der Rache eines schonungslosen Feindes preisgegeben war.

Das Städtchen Lebanon stellt, abgesehen von seiner Geschäftsstraße, einen Haufen über eine rauhe Hochebene unregelmäßig gewürfelter Häuser vor. Bey unserer Ankunft sah es aus, als ob die feindliche Cavallerie vor ihrem Abzug den Boden samt den Häusern auf den Kopf gestellt und ausgeschüttet hätte; alle Wohnungen stunden völlig leer, Einwohner sah man in diesem Lebanon fast ebensowenig als Cedern; in den kleineren Häusern machten es sich jetzt unsere Cavalleristen bequem, und in den paar größeren, stattlicher aussehenden Wohnungen der früheren Aristokratie hatten die Generäle ihre Hauptquartiere aufgeschlagen.

Ende der 19. Manuskriptseite

VI.
Vor dem Feinde. Die ersten Schüsse.

Am Morgen des 10. Febr. brach die Südwest-Armee wieder von Lebanon auf, nachdem daselbst ein Quartiermeister-Depot und ein Feldlazarett errichtet worden waren, und zog auf zwey verschiedenen Straßen auf Springfield zu. Die milde Frühlingssonne ließ uns glauben, daß Winter und Kälte für immer hinter uns lägen, je näher dem sonnigen Süden wir kämen, und leicht und wohlgemuth wie Wanderer im Monat Mai schritten wir über das buschige Hügelland dahin. Ein verhältnismäßig guter Fahrweg brachte uns am Abend des zweiten Tages nach dem Städtchen Marshfield. Hier hatten noch am Morgen vor unserer Ankunft die Vorposten des Feindes gestanden, und von da an bis zur Grenze von Arkansas erwarteten wir täglich, demselben zu begegnen.

Ein buntes Gewirr von Menschen und Wagen bezeichnete am folgenden Morgen den Aufbruch der beyden Sigelschen Divisionen, und es dauerte lange, bis sich der Knäuel gelößt und sich die einzelnen Truppenabtheilungen mit ihrem Wagenzuge in Bewegung gesetzt hatten. „So viel Menschen hat Marshfield noch nie beysammen gesehen", – bemerkte mir im Vorbeigehen ein Bürger mit erzwungenem Lächeln, während er sicherlich uns im

Stillen einen Fluch nachsandte, wenn er auf die rauchenden Trümmer einiger noch während des verzögerten Abmarsches niedergebrannten Häuser oder durch die zerschlagenen Fensterscheiben in die vielen verlassenen Wohnungen blickte, in denen zertrümmert wurde, was zurückgeblieben war. Das vor uns liegende Hügelland begann ein wilderes Aussehen zu gewinnen, und nachmittags kamen wir wieder in ein wirkliches Waldgebirge mit steilen Abhängen und tiefen Schluchten. Die Straße war rauh und durch die schweren Geschütze tief eingeschnitten, der Boden weich, oft so morastig, daß sich unser Fußvolk auf weite Strecken einzeln in den Feldern oder durch

Ende der 20. Manuskriptseite

den Wald einen Weg suchen mußte. Dadurch wurde der Marsch zu einem äußerst langwierigen; bald bleib ein Wagen stecken und mußte durch Vorspann unter unglaublichen Flüchen und Hieben auf das gequälte Vieh wieder flottgemacht werden, bald brach einer zusammen und wurde bey Seite geschafft und abgeladen.

Je weiter wir vorwärts schritten, desto größer wurde die Spannung, womit wir auf das Erscheinen einer Ordonanz oder das Knallen der Geschütze harrten, welches uns das erste Zusammentreffen mit dem Feinde verkünden sollte. Eine auffallende Veränderung läßt sich an einem solchen Tage unter den Truppen beobachten; statt sich wie gewohnt, nach rechts und links sich zu zerstreuen, hinter den Colonen zurückzubleiben oder singend, räisonierend, und Späße treibend vorwärts zu marschieren, blieben sie heute alle schön beysammen und schritten mäuschenstill, nur darauf bedacht, ihre Büchsen in Bereitschaft zu halten, ihres Weges dahin. Es war gegen 4 Uhr Nachmittags, wir durchzogen gerade einen breiten waldigen Bergrücken, als sich vor uns wie aufsteigende Nebel unheimliche schwarze Wolken erhoben, die die sich neigende Sonne verdunkelten; eine immer glühender werdende Hitze, je näher wir kamen, ein brenzlicher Geruch, ein lautes Knistern und Prasseln verriethen uns, daß der Wald vor uns in Brand gerathen war. Durch einen Rauch, der uns kaum zwey Schritte den Weg erkennen ließ und unseren Augen aufs Empfindlichste schmerzte, und eine unerträgliche Glut eilten wir, die Strecke hinter uns zu bringen, wo im Umfang einer Meile, zu beiden Seiten der Straße, die Flammen begierig um sich griffen, indem sie der Wind hastig nach allen Seiten über das dürre Laub und Gras vorwärts trieb, und sie an den niedern Bäumen und Sträuchern, aus denen die hiesigen Wälder bestehen, leicht und zierlich wie Eichhörnchen, heraufglitten und von einem Ast zum andern hüpften.

Ende der 21. Manuskriptseite

Wir hatten heute zwey solche brennenden Waldstrecken zu durchschreiten, bei der zweiten zeigte sich abseits und halb versteckt vor Furcht, wir möchten ihm wehren, ein Bäuerlein, welches einen langen Graben zu ziehen bemüht war, um dadurch dem Feuer eine Grenze zu setzen und es von seiner nahen Farm abzuhalten.

Mit Eintreten der Dunkelheit erreichten wir eine lange Schlucht, die unsern Weg kreuzte; hier sollte unsre Division für diese Nacht rasten, während die erste noch etwas weiter zog. Da unsere Wagen weit zurückgeblieben waren, so nahm auch die Einrichtung des Lagers wenig Zeit in Anspruch; sein Abendbrod fand jeder in seinem Brodsack, falls noch etwas darinn übrig war, und seine Schlafstelle bereitete er sich auf dem steinigen Boden aus zusammengetragenem Laube. Wir hatten uns aber nicht lange auf dem harten Bette zur Ruhe gelegt, als wir durch drei sich rasch folgende Kanonenschüsse aufgeschreckt, durch das Wirbeln unsrer Trommeln zur Sammlung gerufen wurden. Mit einem wahren Freudenjauchzen sprangen unsere Jungen zu den Gewehren und so rüstig und unverdrossen nahmen sie den Marsch wieder auf, als hätten sie mit einem langen Schlaf von dem eben bestandenen ausgeruht. Doch hatten wir nicht viel mehr als eine Meile Weges hinter uns, als Gegenbefehl erschien und wir mit Zurücklassung dreier Companien, welche Vorpostendienst zu versehen hatten, zu unsern Laubbetten zurückkehrten. –

Nach kurzer Ruhe traten wir um 4 Uhr Morgens wieder an. Die Tornister wurden zurückgelassen; nur seinen Brodsack und eine wollene Decke hatte der Soldat umgehängt. Es war noch Nacht; doch der sinkende Mond, dessen Richtung wir folgten, beleuchtete matt unseren Weg über das Waldgebirge, und eine frostige Kälte trieb uns rasch vorwärts. Wir hatten etwa 4 Meilen zurückgelegt, als eine Menge verglimmender Feuer und an den Seiten der Straße einzelne Haufen

Ende der 22. Manuskriptseite

Tornister, sowie Pauken Instrumente uns die Stelle bezeichneten, wo die erste Division, welche aber aufgebrochen war, ihr Nachtlager gehabt hatte. Hier war es auch, wo vorigen Abend die äußersten Vorposten des Feindes, eine Abtheilung Cavallerie, unsere vordersten Truppen mit einigen Flintenschüssen begrüßt hatten und durch jene drei Kartätschenschüsse von unserer Seite, unter Zurücklassung einiger Todter und Verwundeter, verjagt worden waren. Bald brachten uns einzelne zurückkehrende Reiter die weniger unerwartete als unerwünschte Nachricht, daß die gesammte feindliche Armee Springfield geräumt habe und auf dem Rückzug begriffen sey. So zogen wir ohne Schwerdtstreich desselben Morgens in Springfield ein, unsere Division zum zweiten, Sigel zum dritten Mal.

VII.
Einzug ins feindliche Hauptquartier. Brennen und Plündern.

Springfield, der Hauptort des südwestlichen Missouri, war ein hübsches, freundliches Städchen mit manchem stattlichen Frainhaus und wenigen großen Backsteinhäusern, auf einer Höhe gelegen, die sich nach einer Seite in einen Wiesengrund abdacht. In seiner Mitte hatte es wie jede amerikanische Stadt einen großen freyen Platz, an dessen Seite sich ein neues großes steinernes Gebäude, das Rathhaus erhob. Noch immer, wie bey unserer ersten Ankunft leztes Spätjahr, wehte auf diesem Rathhaus die gelbe Fahne, welche es für beyde Armeen als Hospital bezeichnet. So hatte diese gelbe Flagge die beyden anderen Flaggen überdauert, in Springfield und fast in ganz Südmissouri – diese gelbe Flagge, welche das menschliche Elend andeutet, den neutralen Boden, wo der scharfe Stahl in das Fleisch des Feindes wie des Freundes gleich kalt und unbarmherzig einschneidet. Ja wohl war es menschliches Elend, was jeder der feindlichen Brüder hinterlassen; menschliches Elend, was sich auf den Gesichtern der wenigen Einwohner ausdrückte, die wir in den Straßen Springfields

Ende der 23. Manuskriptseite

gewahr wurden. Hier hätte ein Physiognomiker ein reiches Gebiet gehabt, aus den gemischten Zügen dieser geheimen, doch so heiß sprudelnden Regungen des Herzens zu deuten. Neugierde, das Erbstük des Amerikaners, Verwunderung, ob es möglich wäre, dass wir wieder an diesen Platze einzögen, den wir drei Monate lang dem Feinde überlassen hatten, hie und da ein unglückliches Lächeln, unglücklich, weil offenbar erzwungen, als Grundzug aber, der alle andern beherrschte, Furcht und Schrecken – das sprachen zudem beharlich, die Züge der paar Leutchen, die sich ängstlich vor einigen Häusern zeigten oder vorüberhuschten, dieser Leutchen, welche heute uns und gestern unsern Feinde durch ihre kläglichen oder freundlichen Mienen um Schonung für ihr bischen Habe flehten. –

Springfield möchte sonst etwa 6000 Einwohner zählen, jetzt war es wie ausgestorben. Viele Häuser und Scheunen an der Straße, auf welcher wir einzogen, standen leer und offen; ihre Böden waren mit Stroh belegt; offenbar hatten darin Truppen gelegen, und mit großer Wahrscheinlichkeit wurde daraus geschlossen, dass es die Wohnungen geflüchteter Unionsleute waren. Viele andere, darunter sehr stattliche Häuser, inmitten hübscher Gärten, mit den bekannten kleinen Häuschen, den Negerwohnungen, im Hintergrunde zu beiden Seiten des Hofes, schienen gleichfalls unbewohnt zu seyn und waren sichtlich von jeder feindseligen Hand unberührt geblieben; sie wurden als Häuser Südlichgesinnter gedeutet. - Ohne Verzug marschierten wir durch die Stadt und auf der entgegengesetzten Seite derselben heraus. Auf dem Marktplatz trafen wir einen Haufen Gefangene; ohne Waffen oder irgendwelche kriegerische Abzeichen sahen sie aus wie gewöhnliche Farmersjungen. Ebendaselbst ließen wir eine Compagnie für die Provoszwache zurück; von ihren Thätigkeiten gaben freylich die nächstfolgenden Ereignisse einen sehr zweifelhaften Begriff. Denn wir hatten noch nicht lange der Stadt den Rücken gekehrt, als aus einem großen Haus die hellen Flammen aufschlugen, und von da an bis zum nächsten Morgen waren an die zwanzig Häuser und darunter eine

Ende der 24. Manuskriptseite

eine[63] Anzahl der schönsten Privatwohnungen Springfields in Asche gelegt. Mochte nun etwas Wahres daran seyn oder nicht, daß, wie das Gerücht sagte, von Oben herab die Weisung erging, welche Häuser der Zerstörung verfallen waren – gewiß mußte es dem leidenschaftslosen Beurtheilen unbegreiflich erscheinen, warum Eigenthum von Feinden zerstört wurde, wenn man es einmahl in seiner Hand hatte und sich anders zutraute, es behaupten zu können. Wieviele arme Unionsfamilien, welche sich hieher innerhalb die Linien unserer Armee flüchteten, wären glücklich gewesen, in diesen Häusern ein Obdach zu finden. Aber es zeigte sich eben, daß, je länger der Bürgerkrieg dauerte, desto roher und schonungsloser die Kriegsführung wurde. Während der beyden ersten Mahle, daß unsere Truppen Springfield besetzt hatten, war nicht ein einziges Haus zerstört worden, und jetzt innerhalb der ersten zwölf Stunden unmittelbar unter den Augen der Provoßwache und des Obergenerals fiel ein Haus nach dem anderen; war das zufällig? und was wurde aus all dem Hausgeräthe in jenen schönen Häusern, und den reichen Meublen, den schönen Teppichen, den theuren Pianos? Diese waren entweder bey Zeiten von ihren Eigenthümern in Sicherheit gebracht worden, oder sie verbrandten mit oder aber – man glaube nur, die Südländer waren sehr im Unrecht, wenn sie seit der Einnahme von New Oreleans immer und immer wieder behaupteten, die nördlichen Offiziere hätten eine ganz besondere Vorliebe für silbrlne Löffel; die Damen im Norden wollten auch Pianos haben, und Pianos läßt man nicht gern verbrennen. Da war z. B. in unserem Armeecorps

Ende der 25. Manuskriptseite

ein Oberst (er soll in Deutschland Gensdarm gewesen seyn), welcher von seinen Feldzügen in Missouri statt Lorbeeren sowie aber Möblen heimsandte, um damit sein Haus von oben bis unten auf das Reichste und Bequemste auszustatten. Als derselbe später nach einem weit südlicher gelegenen Staate versetzt wurde und seine Ehehälfte zu sich auf Besuch kommen lies, gab er einer dortigen wohlhabenden Familie als Freund den wohlmeinenden Rath, ohne Verzug ihr Haus zu verlassen, weil dasselbe bey dem jeden Augenblick zu erwartenden Angriff in der größten Gefahr stünde; der Angriff erfolgte nicht, aber das würdige Ehepaar zog in die schöne Wohnung ein, machte sich breit darin, und bevor sie dieselbe wieder verließen, wurde alles, was nicht niet- und nagelfest war, in große Kisten verpackt und nach dem fernen Norden verschickt; nicht genung damit, selbst was angewachsen war, schöne Gewächse im Garten wurden ausgegraben und mußte mit, und was nicht nach dem Geschmack des Oberst war, wie namentlich Bücher, das bot er

---

[63] Dieses Wort steht auch am Schluß der vorhergehenden Seite

seinen Herrn Camraden an. „Wir brauchen dies alles nicht für uns, wir haben selber genug –" erzählte die Frau Oberst; „Aber wir haben ein Bäschen, die wird nächstens Hochzeit machen, und da gibt dies gerade eine hübsche Aussteuer für sie." Besagter Oberst galt für einen tüchtigen, nur etwas strengen Militair und er wirkte zuversichtlich, nächstens General zu werden; und doch war dieser Möblenexport nur ein kleinerer Posten auf seinem Sündenregister.

Ende der 25A. Manuskriptseite

VIII.
Ein großmüthiger Feind. Ein räthselhaftes Manöver. Kriegsgräuel.

Auf einer Anhöhe, außerhalb Springfield trafen wir auf eine Menge Baracken, in denen etwa eine Division der feindlichen Armee gelegen haben mochte, dieselben wurden uns als Lager angewiesen, und neugierig machten wir uns daürber her, zu sehen, was für Winterquartiere sich unsere Feinde hergerichtet hätten. Wir fanden diese Baracken wesentlich verschieden, von denjenigen, welche ein Theil unserer Truppen sich bey Rolla erbaut hatte. Die Unsrigen stellten lange bretterne Gebäude vor, so geräumig, daß gut ein halbes Battalion in einer Platz fand; drei übereinander befindliche Pritschen, der Mangel an Licht und Ventillation gaben ihnen große Ähnlichkeit mit dem Zwischendeck eines Auswandererschiffes, sowie einen fruchtbaren Boden für Ungeziefer und Krankheiten. Im Gegensatz dazu waren diese feindlichen Baracken kleine, niedrige Blockhäuser, mit Lehm beworfen und ausgekittet, gut gesichert gegen Wind und Kälte; Entweder waren es längere Gebäude, die durch Wände in vollständig abgesonderte Räume getheilt waren, oder frei stehende kleine Häuschen; alle aber waren sie ausgezeichnet durch hübsche, aus Backsteinen erbaute Kamine, überhaupt so wohnlich eingerichtet wie möglich. Kein Wunder, daß unsere Jungens große Augen machten und davon Veranlassung nahmen, zu raisonniren, denn raisonniren muß der deutsche Soldat und desto mehr, je besser er es hat.

In dem Nebengebäude eines ehemaligen Farmhauses, welches eine Aufschrift als Quartier des Commissärs bezeichnete, fanden wir zu unserer nicht geringen Freude noch einen kleineren Vorrath von Welschkornmehl, frischen Schinken und gedörrtes Obst, gerade genug, daß wir diesen und den nächsten Tag zu leben hatten. Das heißt denn doch: feurige Kohlen aufs Haupt des Feindes sammeln; wir verbrennen den Südländern ihre Häuser, und sie geben uns Obdach und Speise. Wahrlich dieser Price mußte ein humaner, charmanter

Ende der 26. Manuskriptseite

Mann seyn oder – sehr große Eile gehabt haben! Ohne seine Fürsorge hätten wir bey einer eisigen Kälte, die sich von Stunde zu Stunde steigerte, ohne Nahrung den Rest des Tages und die Nacht wiederum unter freiem Himmel zubringen müssen. Denn nur wenige von unsern Wagen erreichten uns an diesem Tage, und diese brachten die Tornister nach und hatten wieder umzukehren, um die unterwegs abgeladene Bagage nachzuholen, mit Ausnahme dessen, was die Fuhrleute zertrümmert hatten oder an der Straße liegenzulassen beliebten. –

Es läßt sich denken, daß unsere Freude nicht gar groß war, als wir nächsten Morgen die warmen Barracken verlassen mußten, um dem Feind nachzujagen, noch bevor unsere Wagen mit Zelten und Proviant uns eingeholt hatten. Es herrschte eine frostige Kälte, ein scharfer Wind blies uns ins Gesicht, der Boden war mit Glatteis bedeckt, und unsere Bärte mit Eiszapfen behangen. Doch trösteten wir uns damit dem Feind in Wilson's Creek, wo es hieß, daß er eine feste Stellung eingenommen hätte, zu begegnen und dort die alte Scharte auszuwetzen; auch ermunterte sich Mancher mit dem schlechten Troste, daß für die feindliche Armee die Kälte ungewohnt und darum empfindlicher wäre. Die waren doppelt betrogen; der Feind bestund fast ausschließlich aus Missouriern, welche dies Clima nicht minder gewohnt waren wie wir, und an eine Schlacht dachte er gar nicht.

Wir waren etwas 2 Meilen weit gegangen, als wir auf einem weiten Felde die erste Division in Schlachtlinie aufgestellt fanden. Auch den Unsrigen wurde ihr Platz als Reserve angewiesen; Generäle und Adjutanten sprengten daher, und alles sah sich begierig nach dem Feinde um. Da gewahrten wir vor uns auf einem Hügel eine lange dunkle Reihe vor einem Gehölze aufgepflanzt; unsere Herren Stabsoffiziere griffen nach ihren Operngläsern und entdeckten, daß es – Fenceriegel waren.

Ende der 27. Manuskriptseite

Nach einer Weile geriethen die Reihen der vor uns stehenden Division in wirre Bewegung; die Kälte trieb die Leute erst herumzuspringen und sich zu boxen, dann aber über eine nahe Fence herzufallen, und Feuer anzumachen. Ein Hauptmann, welcher der mehrstündige Verzug bey solcher Kälte gleich ungeduldig gemacht haben mochte, wandte sich an einen höhern Offizier mit der Frage, warum wir denn nicht vorrückten und erhielt darauf die Antwort: Price ist noch nicht bereit; wir müßten warten, bis er gleichfalls „seine Schlachtlinie aufgestellt hat." Dieser Bescheid möchte weniger zur Erklärung unseres Manövers dienen als zur charakteristisch etwelcher Offiziere unserer freywilligen Armee; denn die Worte waren in vollem Ernste gesprochen, und mit demselben Ernste theilte sie der Hauptmann seiner Compagnie mit.

Dem Stand der Sonne nach – denn unsere Uhren waren längst stehengeblieben – ging es auf Mittag zu, als sich die Schlachtlinie wieder auflöste und der Zug wie gehabt in Bewegung setzte. Ein Weg von 10 (oder 16?) Meilen brachte uns nach Little York, einem kleinen Städchen, was damals aus wenig mehr als 2 kurzen Häuserreihen bestund. Als wir es erreichten, stund das äußerste Haus in Flammen, und wie das Gerücht ging, passierte der letzte Theil unseres Trains nur noch die rauchenden Trümmer des Ortes. Hier hatten Abends zuvor ein paar Companien unserer unermüdlichen deutschen

Cavallerie das Ende des feindlichen Trains aufgejagt und eine bedeutende Zahl Wagen weggenommen und von da nach Springfield zurückgebracht. An der Seite der Straße fanden wir noch die zerschossenen und von Säbelhieben entstellten Leichen einiger bey diesem Anlasse niedergemachten Fuhrleute, blutjunge Burschen und alte Männer, welche mit dem Leben dafür gebüßt, daß sie auf ihren Wagen der feindlichen Armee, d. h. ihren verwandten Freunden das Gepäk nachgeführt hatten. In einem derselben erkannte einer unserer Offiziere einen wohlhabenden alten Farmer und Friedensrichter aus der Nähe der Kansas-Grenze und

Ende der 28. Manuskriptseite

erzählte, wie eines Tages während der blutigen Streitigkeiten, welche kurz vor Ausbruch des Bürgerkrieges die Grenzbewohner von Missouri und Kansas miteinander geführt, jener Alte bey seiner Heimkehr sein Haus von Kansasleuten überfallen, seinen Sohn erhängt und seine Frau mißhandelt und halb wahnsinnig gefunden hätte. Jetzt war also auch noch das Haupt der Familie dem Fluch der Sclaverei zum Opfer gefallen.

Ein paar Meilen außerhalb Little York wurde auf einer weiten, steinigen Heide halt gemacht und den verschiedenen Truppenabtheilungen ihr Lagerplatz für die kommende Nacht angewiesen. Ein unfreundlicheres Lager hatten wir noch nie gehabt. Ein zerfallenes, kleines Blockhaus wurde zum Hauptquartier gemacht, darin der General mit seinem Stabe residierte. Dicht daneben, in einem spärlichen niederen Gehölz, wenn es diesen Namen verdiente, suchten unsere Truppen Schutz vor dem scharfen Winde. Die Kälte, welche durch die Mittagssonne etwas gemildert worden war, erreichte wieder die frühere eisige Höhe. Nur ein einziger Wagen mit einigen Zelten hatte uns eingeholt. Holz für Feuer war, wie angedeutet, spärlich. Die Lebensmittel bestunden hauptsächlich aus einigen Schafen, Kälbern und Gänsen, die uns bey Little York in den Weg gelaufen und als Kriegsgefangene mitgeschleppt worden waren. –

IX.

Unser Lebenselixier. Weite Märsche und wenig Schlaf. Künftige Lagerung und Brandstätten.

Am Morgen nach der durchfrorenen Nacht erschienen noch rechtzeitig vor dem Aufbruche einige unserer Wagen, welche die Tornister und so viel Proviant brachten, daß es möglich wurde, jedem Soldaten einen Becher heißen Kaffees und ein paar Zwieback zu reichen. Es war dies die einzige Nahrung, welche vor Abend zu haben war, und für Manchen das Einzige, was er an Nahrung seit gestern Morgen zu sich genommen hatte. Zwieback oder

Ende der 29. Manuskriptseite

hartes Brodt ersetzte in der amerikanischen Armee das Kommisbrod und hat vor diesem den Vorzug, daß er besser schmeckt und weniger leicht verdirbt; es ist eine gute Qualität von weißem Schiffszwieback, in viereckigen Tafeln, oft steinhart, aus gutem Weizenmehl gebacken und war bisher immer in reichlicher Menge geliefert worden. Das Werthvollste aber, was der amerikanische Soldat erhält, ist der Kaffe, welcher, entweder grün oder geröstet, bisher immer in genügender Quantität und von guter Sorte bezogen wurde. Einmahl erhielten wir statt seiner versuchsweise ein dickflüssiges Extrakt, welches die Bestandtheile von Kaffe, Milch und Zucker concentriert enthalten sollte, sich aber durchaus nicht bewährte. Der Kaffe ist ein Ersatz für geistige Getränke, welche in der Armee und Flotte der vereinigten Staaten nicht geliefert wurden und sogar verbothen sind, und mit Recht! Denn einerseits gilt was die Leute nicht an den Brandtwein zu gewöhnen, was um so nöthiger, da der Amerikaner und der Irrländer im Trinken kein Maas kennt und in der regulären Armee die Trunksucht ohnehin ein Krebsschaden ist, woran Offiziere und Soldaten leiden; andererseits überzeugten wir uns, daß der Kaffe nachhaltiger, belebender und wärmender wirkt als der Brandtwein. Mit seinem Becher Kaffe im Leibe und ein paar Stüke Zwieback im Brodsack, bepackt mit Tornister, wollener Decke, Brodsack, Feldflasche und mit einem Beil oder Kessel, marschierte unser Soldat den ganzen Tag durch Frost und Regen, durchwatete Bäche und kleinere Flüsse, deren Wasser ihm oft bis fast an die Brust ging, und machte in der Regel keinen längeren Halt bis er Abends auf dem Lagerplatz ankam, und hatte er sich hier erst am Feuer getrocknet und durch einen Becher Kaffe erwärmt, so fühlte er sich wieder neu belebt und zog unverdrossen auf die Wache oder gab sich mit einem solchen Wohlbehagen der Ruhe und dem Genuß einer Pfeife Tabak hin, daß es mir oft vorkam, ich hätte mich noch nie nach einer Mahlzeit wohler gefühlt als nach derjenigen, welche soeben, mein Mittag- und Abendbrod zugleich gebildet, aus Kaffe, Zwieback und einem Stück gebratenen Schinken oder Speck bestanden hatte.

Auch heute that der Kaffe seine Wunder, er stärkte uns zum weitesten Tagesmarsch, den wir auf diesem Feldzug zurückgelegt hatten. Wir marschierten ununterbrochen bis 4 Uhr Nachmittags. Das Wetter begünstigte uns, die Sonne schien den

Ende der 30. Manuskriptseite

ganzen Tag, und wir hatten für einige Tage wieder das schönste Frühlingswetter. So fanden wir den Winter im ganzen Süden, vom Missouri-Fluss bis hinunter an den Golf von Mexiko; erst 3–8 Tage milde Wärme, dann Gewitter und Regen und damit der Eintritt einer empfindlichen Kälte, welche zwey bis drei Tage anhält.

Wie freudig begrüßten wir an diesem Abend die Ankunft unserer lange vermißten Wagen! wie eifrig fielen wir über ihre Vorräthe her, um daraus ein solides Mahl herzurichten und uns gründlich zu sättigen! Da kam der Befehl, keine Zelte aufzuschlagen, wohl aber tüchtig zu kochen und unsere Brodsäcke für den nächsten Tag zu füllen, sich sodann früh aufs Ohr zu legen und bereit zu halten, um gleich nach Mitternacht wieder aufzubrechen. Es war zwey Uhr, als am nächsten Morgen angetreten wurde, dauerte aber noch eine volle Stunde, bis der Zug in Gang war. Denn täglich, bey jedem Aufbruch wiederholte es sich, daß wir den Weg vor uns durch noch ungeordnete Regimenter und durch einen Knäuel von Wagen gesperrt fanden, oder daß wir immer wieder Halt machen und Cavallerie und Artillerie vorbeilassen mußten. Nichts ermüdet aber die Truppen mehr als ein solcher Verzug, und ein solcher kam nicht nur während des Aufbruchs vor, sondern auch häufig genug während des Marsches. Es offenbarte sich eben auch hierin wie in Allem der Mangel an Organisation, Übung und Disciplin, welcher die Amerikanische Armee bezeichnet. Die Truppen wurden abgemüdet, litten oft am Nothwendigsten und doch waren ihre Bewegungen schwerfällig und langsam. Was Wunder, daß uns Price mit seinen leichtfüßigen Missouriern entwischte. Sie hatten ursprünglich nur 6–8 Stunden Vorsprung vor uns, und doch war es unserer aus Cavallerie und reitender Artillerie bestehenden Vorhut bis heute noch nicht gelungen, auch nur die Nachhut des Feindes zum Stehen zu bringen.

Ein zweiter Fehler bey unseren Märschen war der, daß keine regelmäßige, längere Rast gemacht wurde; mit Ausnahme jener unfreiwilligen, nur ermüdenden Verzögerungen ging es unaufhaltsam von Morgens früh bis Abends von einem Lagerplatz zum anderen. Für heute hatte dies sein Gutes; denn uns alle drückte eine solche Schlaftrunkenheit, daß, wer sich für einen Augenblick

Ende der 31. Manuskriptseite

niedersetzte, auch sofort einschlief und nur mit Gewalt aufgerüttelt werden konnte. Halb schlafend marschierten die Soldaten; mein Pferd hing den Kopf und tappte mit geschlossenen Augen mitten unter dem Fußvolk, und ich hing den Kopf mit ihm und schreckte alle zehn Minuten auf, wenn mein nikender Kopf mich aus der Balance bringen wollte. In einem Gehölze, welches sich eine Strecke weit längs der Straße erhob, lagen überall unser schlafende Krieger, oft in Gruppen unter einem überragenden Felsblocke gelagert wie die Siebenschläfer in ihrer Höhle, einem so tiefen Schlummer verfallen, daß der ärgste Tumult auf der Straße sie nicht aufzuwecken im Stande war.

Es ist in der amerikanischen Armee Regel, daß nach drei Tage Marsches ein Rasttag gehalten wird. Auf unserem gegenwärtigen Verfolgungszug wurde diese Regel nicht beachtet; um uns aber wenigstens einen halben Tag Ruhe zu geben, wurde heute schon um 2 Uhr gelagert. Hier holte uns auch unser Train wieder ein und gab uns zum ersten Mahl seit fünf Tagen Gelegenheit, unter unsern Zelten zu schlafen.

Unser diesmaliger Lagerplatz war am Anfang einer anmuthigen, dichter besiedelten und wohl angebauten Landschaft gelegen; vor uns dehnte sich ein weites Wiesenthal aus, begrenzt von waldigen Höhen und durchzogen von einem Bache, welcher mehrere Mühlen trieb, und von der Landstraße, an welcher viele kleinere und einige größere Bauernhöfe und zwey Städchen lagen. Das erste dieser Städchen, Cassville genannt bestund aus mehreren Straßen mit vielen Kaufläden und anderen Geschäftslokalen und hatte in seiner Mitte ein großes, steinernes Rathhaus. Das zweite über eine Meile vom ersteren entfernte Städtchen bestund aus wenig mehr als einer einzigen Reihe bescheidener Holzhäuser und einem großen stattlichen aber gleichfalls aus Holz gebauten Hause mit weitem Gehöfe, nach dessen Besitzer, einem Herrn Keats[64], der Ort den Namen Keatsville führte, wie es denn vielfach im Westen Sitte ist, daß Städe und Fleken nach ihrem ältesten und reichsten Ansiedler benannt werden.

Ende der 32. Manuskriptseite

Jetzt stunden die meisten Häuser dieser beyden Ortschaften leer; drei Wochen später waren sie alle dicht bevölkert und zwar von den Verwundeten unserer Armee. In der Kirche und in den kleinen Holzhäusern von Keatsville lagen unsere verwundeten Deutschen, auf Stroh gelagert, jeden Comfort entbehrend, aber sich eines verhältnißmäßig trefflichen Gesundheitszustandes erfreuend. Nach Casville wurden die verwundeten Amerikaner geschafft, auch viele andere Kranke derselben, und füllten dort die weiten Räume des Rathhauses und andere größere Gebäude; ihre Zahl war viel beträchtlicher, ihre Versorgung besser, weil die von St. Louis kommenden Hospital- und sonstigen Vorräthe ihnen als den zunächst gelegenen zuerst in die Hände fielen. Dagegen hatte ihre Anhäufung in einzelnen großen Lokalen sowie das Zusammenliegen von Verwundeten und Typhuskranken die Folge, daß Pyämie und Typhus in schrecklichem Grade um sich griffen und ein Jahr später, als längst das Spital aufgehoben und das Städtchen selber,#[65] durch den Vandalismus einer zweiten Unionsarmee in Asche gelegt war, ein weiter Friedhof die Stätte bezeichnete, wo einst Cassville gestanden und die Verwundeten von Pearidge ein Asyl gefunden hatten.

X.
Raubritter. Auf der Grenze von Arkansas. Ein künftiges und ein frisches Schlachtfeld.

Durch das eben beschriebene Wiesenthal und seine beiden Ortschaften ging folgenden Tages unser Marsch. Dabei ereignete sich vor unseren Augen ein kleiner Zwischenfall, welcher deßhalb erwähnt werden mag, weil er an einen der schwarzen Punkte in unserem Soldatenleben erinnert, nemlich an

---

[64] Ursprünglich „Ceats" geschrieben; das „C" wurde dann mit einem „K" überschrieben.
[65] Bemerkung am Rand der Seite: „Ebenso wie Keatsville"

den Pferdediebstahl, den sich gelegentlich Gemeine und Offiziere erlaubten, und wobey weder Freund noch Feind
Ende der 33. Manuskriptseite
verschont wurde, nicht einmahl die Privatpferde der eigenen Offiziere.

Diesen Nachmittag kam nemlich ein älterer Landmann auf einem mittelmäßigen Pferde unserer Colonne entgegen; ritt über den Rand der Straße hinunter und bog ehrerbietig vor uns und etwaigen Kolbenstößen so weit aus, als es nur das Terrain erlaubte. Allein ein Offizier hatte ihn ins Auge gefaßt, ritt auf ihn zu, rief noch ein paar Soldaten herbei und zwang den verblüfften Reiter abzusteigen, indem er behauptete, ein altes, verwischtes Brandzeichen, welches am ehesten ein O vorgestellt haben mochte, beweise, daß das Thier zur rebellen Armee gehört hätte. Der Landmann betheuert, das Pferd sey immer sein Eigenthum gewesen, und das Zeichen könne ja ganz unmöglich ein CS – das Zeichen der Confederierten Staaten – gewesen seyn. Umsonst! Der Bursche des Offizieres schwingt sich in den Sattel und trabt mit dem Gaul von dannen, und der Offizier erzählte mit vergnügtem Lachen, wie er jetzt ein Pferd mehr habe. Der Farmer aber springt unterdessen längs der Straße der Colonne voraus und wendet sich dort an ein paar Offiziere; allein während er diesen sein Leid klagt, wittert Jemand in der Nähe einen Revolver in seiner Tasche. „Halloh, Bursche! Ihr tragt ja Waffen bey Euch; Heraus damit!" – und wohl oder wehe – auch noch der Revolver mußte abgeliefert werden. „Und jetzt macht Euch aus dem Staube, [...][66] ... Rebell! Schnell! Fort mit Euch, oder ..." Dem also gerupften blieb nichts Anderes übrig, als sich schleunigst in die Büsche zu schlagen. Aber ein Bauer gibt einen Handel so leicht nicht auf, auch in Amerika nicht. So ein nemlicher Farmer war bisher gewohnt, gegen einen Pferdedieb die ganze Nachbarschaft aufzubiethen und den Eingefangenen allenfalls mit eigener Hand an einem Baum aufzuknüpfen. Und jetzt sollte er sich sein Pferd zwischen den Beinen wegstehlen lassen? Nein; Abends in unserem Lager tauchte plötzlich
Ende der 34. Manuskriptseite

der Alte wieder auf, wandte sich mit seinen Klagen an den General und erhielt sein Pferd zurück.

Einige Meilen jenseits des lezten Städtchens stiegen wir in eine tiefe Schlucht hinab, welche sich, erst enger, dann immer breiter werdend, mehrere Meilen weit zwischen hohen Bergrücken hinzog. An dem abschüssigen Rande, der rauhen Straße und oft quer halb darüber lagen mächtige Baumstämme, offenbar hatten damit unsere Feinde den Weg blockirt um unser Vorrücken für ein paar Stunden zu verzögern, und unsere Vorhut hatte sie nothdürftig auf die Seite geschafft. Hier lag die Grenze von Missouri und

---

[66] Dieses Wort ist unleserlich, und könnte „verd" oder „yard" heißen.

Arkansas. Als wir eben dieselbe überschritten, erscholl aus den Bergen vor uns das Krachen schwerer Geschütze; Schuß folgte auf Schuß und rollte wie ferner Donner durch die Schluchten und Berge. Nach einer guten halben Stunde wurde es wieder still, die Dämmerung brach herein, und wir lagerten zum Ersten mal auf dem Boden von Arkansas. Den folgenden Morgen führte uns der Weg an das entgegengesetzte Ende des Thales und dann eine steile Höhe hinauf. Hier dehnte sich zu beiden Seiten der Straße eine weite Hochebene vor uns aus, meist offenes, bebautes Land und mitunter eine kleine Strecke Wald. Zunächst traffen (sic!) wir rechts an der Straße ein großes, von Holz gebautes Gasthaus, Elkhorn Tavern genannt, dahinter und längs der Straße hin ein schmales, lichtes Gehölze und rechts davon eine jähe Fluh, welche mit hohen Bäumen bewachsen und mit einzelnen riesigen Felsblöcken bedeckt, den höchsten Punkt dieser Landschaft bildete und Pea Ridge hieß. Darnach nannten wir, nach jenem Gasthofe dagegen nannten die Südlichen die Schlacht, welche vierzehn Tage später in dieser Gegend geschlagen und auf diesem Punkte entschieden wurde.

Unsere Landstraße führte uns nun eine lange Strecke über die Hochebene; dann ging sie wieder einen steilen, waldigen Abhang hinunter in ein tiefes

Ende der 35. Manuskriptseite

Thal, welches, ähnlich dem eben durchwanderten, in einer Länge von 6–8 Meilen das Hochland von Ost nach West durchschnitt. Mitten durch dieses Thal schlängelte sich ein Bach, „Zukerbach" genannt an demselben theilt sich die Straße, indem ihr einer Arm das Thal der Länge nach durchzieht während der andere quer durch dasselbe und den gegenüberliegenden niedrigen Bergrand hinauf läuft. An dieser Stelle war gestern Abend unsere Vorhut auf den Nachtrab des Feindes gestoßen, und es hatte sich ein kleines Scharmützel entsponnen, aus dem sich, wie es schien, der Feind gut herausgezogen hatte; wenigstens ließ er weder Todte noch Verwundete in unseren Händen. Auf und neben der Straße fanden wir eine Anzahl todter Pferde, und in einem nahen Hause lagen unsere Gefallenen, elf an der Zahl, ausgestellt. Ich erkannte darunter keinen alten Bekannten, wohl aber mit Leichtigkeit aus den Gesichtern der Todten die Nationalität, der jeder angehörte: hier aus dem schmalen, länglichen Gesichte, dem langgestreckten Halse, der scharf geschnittenen Nase und den schmalen Lippen den Amerikaner, dort das runde, volle Gesicht des Deutschen, und daneben den rothen Krauskopf des Irrländers mit dem starken Unterkiefer, den breiten Backenknochen und der Stumpfnase. Unsere weniger Verwundeten waren in einem nahen Blockhause untergebracht, dessen Insassen ihre bescheidenen Räumlichkeiten mit ihnen theilen mußten; zum Dank dafür wurde 14 Tage später dies Haus niedergebrannt – aus strategischen Rücksichten, hieß es.

Auf den Wiesen längst des Zucker-Baches schlugen wir unsere Lager auf und hielten den folgenden Tag einen Rasttag, der um so erwünschter kam, als ein Regen und abends Frost eintrat. Während dieser Rast ereignete sich einer jener Unfälle, wie sie bey der Sorglosigkeit unserer Soldaten nicht eben selten waren. Zwei unserer Leute machten dicht vor ein paar Munitionskisten ein Feuer an und setzten sich rauchend und plaudernd auf die Kisten, um sich am Feuer zu wärmen. Plötzlich erfolgte ein Knall, und unsere Krieger flogen in die Luft und in einen nahen Graben. Ohne schweren Schaden genommen zu haben, aber mit verbrannten Kleidern und an Gesicht und Händen schwarz wie Neger wurden sie von ihren Kameraden aufgehoben,

Ende der 36. Manuskriptseite

und zu den übrigen Verwundeten in jenes Blockhaus gebracht, von wo sie ein paar Wochen später gehärtet und durch viele kleine, blaue Punkte gekennzeichnet zurückkehrten.

XI.

Uebel berüchtigter Feind. Räuberbanden. Land und Leute in Arkansas.

Während so die Infanterie am Zuckerbach lag, durchstreifte unsere Cavallerie unter General Asboth die Gegend vor uns und nahm zunächst vom Städtchen Bentonville Besitz, dem Hauptort des nordwestlichsten Bezirkes von Arkansas. Hier hatte bisher der südliche General Mac Cullock sein Hauptquartier gehabt, derselbe welcher zusammen mit Price lezten Sommer die Unionsarmee unter General Lyons bey Wilsons Creek geschlagen hatte. Ben Mac Cullock war ein gefürchteter Mann, eine fast mythische Figur; er war einer jener Trapper oder Grenzbewohner von Texas, deren Leben eine Reihe von Abendtheuern und Kämpfen mit Indianern und Mexikanern bildet, und genoß den Ruf, der verwegenste und geschickteste Anführer jener Trapper zu seyn. Mit seinem Namen und den von ihm angeführten Truppen aus Texas und Arkansas dräuten zu Anfang des Krieges südliche Zeitungen wie mit Schreckbildern von Unholden und Riesen. Denn die Bewohner von Texas und Arkansas genossen in den Staaten und in alten Romanen den Ruf, die gefährlichsten aller Grenzstrolche zu seyn und wurden nie anders gedacht als mit einem Bowiemesser, einer Schnapsflasche und einem Revolver in jeder Tasche ihrer zerlumpten Kleidung. Allein werden solche Leute nicht als selbständige Truppenkörper verwendet, sondern einer größeren Armee einverleibt so wird ihre Unbändigkeit sehr bald gebrochen, und militärische Ordnung und Gleichförmigkeit verwischen ihre Eigenthümlichhkeiten. So geschah es mit den gefürchteten Truppen des Mac Cullocks. Er selber genoß große Popularität unter den Seinigen und alle Achtung bey uns, da er seine Gefangenen sehr gut behandelte. Die Texanische Infanterie erwarb sich den Ruf

Ende der 37. Manuskriptseite

großer Tapferkeit sowohl im fernen Virginien unter ihrem General Hood als im Westen; wo namentlich bey der von ihnen vergeblich versuchten Erstürmung von Corinth ihr Heldenmuth die Bewunderung sowohl der siegreichen Armee des General Rosecranz als des ganzen Nordens gewann.

Die Texanische Reiterei, Texasrangers genannt, ausgezeichnet durch ihre kleinen, äußerst ausdauernden Pferde, die „Texanischen Ponnies," fanden von Anfang an in der südlichen Reiterei Kameraden, die ihnen an Muth und Verwegenheit gleichkamen. Ganz unbegründet fanden wir jenes Vorurtheil in Bezug auf die Truppen und die Bewohner von Arkansas im Allgemeinen. Wohl aber tauchte hier um diese Zeit eine Klasse von Menschen auf, welche den hergebrachten Ruf mehr als rechtfertigten und seither der Schrecken des nördlichen Arkansas und des waldigen, theils gebirgigen, theils sumpfigen Grenzdistrikts von Missouri waren, nemlich förmlich organisierte Banden von Räubern und Mordbrennern, zusammengesetzt aus alten Desperados und Pferdedieben von hier und Kansas und bekannt unter dem Namen „Jayhawkers". Sie gehörten keiner Parthei an; mit der größten Unpartheilichkeit brandschatzten sie Unionsleute und Südlich gesinnte gleichmäßig; ihre Politik war, Pferde und Maulthiere zu stehlen und gelegentlich auch anderweitig zu rauben und zu brandschatzen. Überall, wo weder nördliche noch südliche Truppen in der Nähe waren, tauchten sie auf und nahmen den armen Leuten, was jene ihnen noch gelassen. ## Nach Beendigung des Krieges, als die südlichen Soldaten nach Hause kehrten und nördliche Garnisonen im Land umher lagen, verschwanden mit Einem mahl die „Jayhawkers". Mancher von ihnen fühlte sich bey der Berührung mit den Heimgekehrten beengt oder gründlich am Halse zusammengeschnürt, und das veranlaßte Jeden, der noch Zeit hatte in den fernen Territorien oder im weiten Texas eine Luftveränderung vorzunehmen!

Auch jenseits des Mississippi, im westlichen Tenessee, hausten solche Banden, welche dort hauptsächlich aus Deserteuren der südlichen Armee bestunden und fälschlich Guerillas genannt wurden. (Dicht vor Memphis
Ende der 38. Manuskriptseite

und seinen nördlichen Vorposten trieben sie dort ihr Unwesen, überfielen oder beraubten Jeden, der ihnen in die Hände kam, brannten Häuser nieder, erschossen oder erhängten ihre Bewohner, schlugen sogar oder peitschten Neger förmlich zu Tode – kurz, verübten alle Schandthaten, welche ihnen Raubsucht, Grausamkeit und Privatrache eingaben.)
 Unser nächster Tagemarsch[67] führte erst durch die ganze Länge des Wiesenthales und dann allmählig aufsteigend in eine hochgelegene, wellenförmige Landschaft, wo prächtige Wälder, weite wohlbebaute Felder und Wiesen, mehrere Ortschaften und große, stattliche Bauernhöfe einen überraschend freundlichen Anblick boten und zu erkennen gaben, daß wir uns nicht mehr in Missouri, sondern in einem ganz anderen Land befanden. 16–18 Meilen vom lezten Lagerplatze und etwa 3 Meilen südöstlich von

---

[67] In den Notizen dieser Abschrift wird der 20. Februar als jener Tag angegeben.

Städtchen Bentonville schlugen wir unsere Zelte auf, und hier, auf einem niedern, flachen Hügel unter Obstbäumen gelagert, genossen wir bey ununterbrochen schönem Frühlingswetter eine Rast von 8 Tagen, nachdem unser Feldzug gerade 3 Wochen gedauert hatte. Jetzt und noch mehr zwei Monate später, als wir weit östlich von hier zum zweiten Mal den Boden von Arkansas betraten, überraschte uns auf das Angenehmste der Unterschied in Bezug auf Land und Leute hier und in Süd-Missouri. Ja, unsre Farmerjungen aus dem gepriesenen Illinois rissen ihre Augen groß auf; das war freylich eine andere Natur als ihre so fruchtbaren, aber auch so unsäglich langweiligen Prairien. Wo gibt es dort wo überhaupt jenseits des Mississippi solche Wälder und einen solchen Reichthum an Quellen, Bächen und Flüssen vom klarsten Wasser und reich an Fischen! Wir jauchzten laut auf und glaubten in der alten Heimath zu seyn, wenn wir durch diese Urwälder mit ihren mächtigen, stolzen Stämmen und dem üppigen Laubwerke ritten; und wie staunten wir, wenn wir dann plötzlich vor einer weiten Lichtung stunden und eine große Farm vor uns lag, ein ungeheures, umzäuntes Viereck von wohlbebauten Feldern, Obstgärten und Wiesen samt Wohnungen und Gehöfe. Es ist dies eine Eigenthümlichkeit von Arkansas, daß einzelne große Farmen oder Complexe von kleineren mitten im

Ende der 39. Manuskriptseite

Walde gelegen sind, und war für uns immer ein überaus lieblicher Anblick, vom hohen, dunkeln Waldessaum umschlossen und vom blauen Himmel überwölbt diese weiten hellgrünen Felder zu sehen. Noch schöner muß der Farbencontrast im Spätjahr seyn, wenn die Baumwolle wie Schnee die Felder bedeckt. Die hiesigen Landprodukte sind außer Baumwolle, welche mehr nur für den Hausbedarf gebaut wird, Weizen und Welschkorn, welche seit Ausbruch des Krieges die Baumwolle vollends fast verdrängten und außerdem Tabak, Kartoffeln, besonders die s.g. süßen Kartoffeln und eine schwere Menge Obst, namentlich Aepfel und Pfirsiche und in der Nähe von Little Rock der weiße amerikanische Wein, welcher von deutschen Bauern aus der Catawba Rebe gewonnen wird und noch die meiste Aehnlichkeit mit dem Moselwein hat. Große Baumwollenplantagen gibt es hier keine dieselben liegen weiter südlich in den Sumpfgegenden längs der großen Flüsse. Hier im nördlichen Theile von Arkansas, sowohl auf den Waldfarmen als auf den weiten offenen Landstrecken, welche, wie bey Bentonville, alle cultivirt sind, wohnt daher nicht die eigentliche s.g. Sclavenhalteraristokratie, sondern ein mehr oder weniger wohlhabender Bauernstand, welcher alles selber zieht, was er bedarf. Diese Leute wie auch die Bewohner von Südmissouri sind fast alles Eingewanderte meistens aus Kentucky und dies sind die aufgeklärtesten und gewandtesten – und aus jenen armen Gebirgsgegenden der Südstaaten, Ost-Tennessee, Nord-Carolina und dem nördlichen Georgia. Farbige kamen uns wenige zu Gesicht, mit Ausnahme alter, schwächlicher Haussklaven und Kindern waren sie alle ebenso wie Vieh oder Pferde nach dem Süden getrieben worden. Auch die weiße männliche Bevölkerung, wenigstens alle jüngeren Männer, waren von Hause fort, wo? ließ sich leicht errathen; dagegen waren Frauen und Kinder meist zurückgeblieben, um durch ihre Gegenwart ihr Eigenthum zu schützen. Ja, im östlichen Theil von Nord-Arkansas, wo wir später einrückten,

Ende der 40. Manuskriptseite

war auch ein großer Theil der jüngeren Männer zu Hause geblieben; viele derselben hatten sich vor den südlichen Conscriptions-Offizieren geflüchtet gehabt und kamen jetzt zu Hunderten nach unserm Hauptquartier vor, um den Eid der Treue gegen die Vereinigten Staaten zu leisten, und die darauf bezügliche Bescheinigung in Empfang zu nehmen; durch dieselbe waren sie gegen Confiscation und Acquisitionen sicher gestellt, und geschah es dennoch, daß die Armee ihrer Vorräthe bedurfte, so erhielten sie für das Gelieferte eine Geldanweisung an die Regierung, welche bey einem Quartiermeister oder Regierungsbeamten eingelöst oder auch wie ein Wechsel verkauft werden konnte.

Fast jeden Tag durchstreifte ich, allein oder in Begleitung eines Kameraden, die Umgegend und stieg vor dem einen oder anderen der hübschen Farmhäuser ab, die durch ihr gefäliges Aussehen wieder ganz an Illinois erinnerten. Meine Absicht war, theils Land und Leute kennenzulernen, theils Nahrungsmittel, Eyer, dürres Obst, süße Kartoffeln einzuhandeln. Gewöhnlich gelang es meiner freundlichen Anrede und dem Vorweisen von Silbermünzen – dem Vereinigten-Staaten Papiergeld trauten sie noch nicht –, die Scheu und den Argwohn der Hausbewohner zu verscheuchen; ließ sie dagegen ihre feindliche Gesinnung auf der Aussage beharren, sie hätten Nichts, so griff ich zum lezten Mittel, was seinen Eindruck auf die Frauen nie verfehlte; ich holte aus einer der beyden Ledertaschen, welche nach Landessitte zu beyden Seiten meines Sattels hingen, ein Säckchen Kaffee hervor, dieses Lieblingsgetränk aller Frauen, welches seit Beginn des Krieges eine Seltenheit und nur für schweres Geld zu haben war. Das Rasseln mit diesem Sake, der Anblick der langentbehrten Kaffeebohnen, wie sie über den Tisch rollten, wirkte immer wie eine Wünschelruthe, in einer halben Stunde war der Tisch gedeckt mit allem, was Küche und Speisekammer aufzuweisen hatten; und mir lachte wieder ein Mal ein weisses, sauberes Tischtuch und blankes Geschirr entgegen

Ende der 41. Manuskriptseite

und darauf die Speisen, welche für einen Soldaten ein Festessen, für den Farmer alltäglich waren, frische Milch, noch dampfende kleine Weißbrödchen, ein Stück gebratenes Geflügel, Eyerspeisen, Gemüse und was auf dem amerikanischen Farmertische nie fehlte, frich gebackener Maiskuchen und als Zubehör dazu, Butter und Molasses (ein aus dem Zuckerrohr bereiteter

Syrup). Auch gesprächig wurden die Frauen, wenn sie uns nach der Mahlzeit Stühle neben sich vor dem Kamin anbothen und anfingen, mit Behaglichkeit ihre Pfeifen zu rauchen. Das Tabakrauchen nemlich, welches im Norden nur selten bey Frauen und nur bey Irländerinnen vorkommt, ist im Süden allgemeine Sitte unter den Frauen auf dem Lande namentlich unter den älteren, selbst wohlhabenderen; jedoch keineswegs unter den reichen Pflanzerinnen. Der Tabak ist selbst gezogen; die Pfeife besteht aus einem Stück Schilfrohr und einem Thonkopf oder in Ermangelung dessen auch wohl einem ausgehöhlten Maiskolben. Diese Frauen in Nord-Arkansas gehörten mit zu den besten, die ich in Amerika kennenlernte, zu jenem, vortrefflichen Schlage der amerikanischen Farmers-Frauen welche ebensoweit verschieden sind von jener betörten Klasse fauler, anspruchsvoller, gezierter und schwächlicher Ladies der Städte und Städtchen in Nord und Süd als von den nicht weniger faulen, in höchstem Grade ungebildeten, überhaupt höchst unseligen Weibern der armen weißen Bevölkerung in den Baumwollenstaaten – gesund und kräftig, schlicht und thätig wie unsere deutschen Bäuerinnen, aber gewandter im Gespräch und im geselligen Umgang, sind sie Meisterinnen in der Hauswirtschaft und zeichnen sich aus durch eine Ordnungsliebe und Sauberkeit, die unübertrefflich ist. Hier in Arkansas wie auch anderwärts im Süden gehört zu den weiblichen Arbeiten eine welche die nördliche Farmerin nicht kennt, in jedem einigermaßen wohlhabenden Hause sah ich nemlich einen Webstuhl, an welchem die Frauen aus der selbstgepflanzten Baumwolle Tuch woben; dieses färbten

Ende der 42. Manuskriptseite

färbten[68] sie mit Eichenrinde und verfertigten daraus eigenhändig die Kleider für ihre Männer, Kinder und Sklaven, jene grobe, aber solide, röthlich-gelbe Kleidung, welche von der männlichen Landbevölkerung des Südens vorwiegend und während des Krieges ausschließlich getragen wurde.

XII.
Soldaten Wirthschaft. Die Geißel des Krieges. Eine Vergiftung und ihre Folgen.

In diesem schönen Arkansas also lagen wir unter unsern Obstbäumen und pflegten der Ruhe; das Land aber zahlte die Zeche. Unser mitgeführter Proviant war zu Ende und frische Zufuhr spärlich, die Texas-Rangers waren in unseren Rücken gekommen und hatten einen großen Proviantzug theils zerstört, theils weggenommen. Dies nöthigte uns, kleine Streifcorps mit leeren Wagen auszusenden, um auf Vorräthe zu fahnden, welche bisweilen in großen Gruben oder unter Heuschobern versteckt gefunden wurden. Mit Schweinen, Schinken, Weizen und Welschkornmehl und Futter für unsere Thiere kehrten dieselben gewöhnlich zurück; manchmal brachten sie auch

---

[68] „färbten" ist am Anfang der Seite 43 wiederholt.

süße Kartoffeln und ein paar Mal große Wagenladungen der schönsten Äpfel. Da wurde dann darauflos geschlachtet, gebradten und gebacken; wo man nur durch ein Lager schritt, begegnete man wahren Schanzen von Fladen[69], welche aus Mehl und Schweinsfett mit oder ohne Apfel gebacken waren und Brod oder Zwieback ersetzen mußten. Kaffee dazu fehlte; statt seiner trank fast alles den rothen Thee von Sassafrasholz; dieser genießt sonst in der Medizin und noch mehr unter dem Volk, wo er zu Hause ist, den Ruf eines Blutreinigungsmittels; jetzt, seit Kaffee und Thee aus dem Lande verschwunden waren, wurde er zum allgemeinen Volksgetränk in Arkansas, und auch unsere Soldaten und Offiziere sammelten eifrig dieses in den dortigen Wäldern reichlich wuchernde Gesträuch und schmeichelten sich dabey, mit dem Angenehmen das Nützliche zu verbinden und aus der Noth eine Frühlingskur zu machen.

Während sich so unsere Infanterie häuslichen Geschäften und der Gesundheitspflege

Ende der 43. Manuskriptseite

hingab und das Land auf eine Weise aussog, welche im Kriege für erlaubt gilt, war unsere Reiterei unermüdlich im Recognoscieren und schwang mit schonungsloser Hand die Kriegsgeißel über der unglücklichen Gegend. Das hübsche Städchen Bentonville war ihr erstes Opfer. Als unsere Cavallerie davon Besitz genommen und es gleich darauf wieder verlassen hatte, soll ein Soldat zurückgeblieben und seine Leiche bey der zweiten Ankunft unserer Truppen aufgefunden worden sein. Es gelang weder mir noch meinen Freunden auszufinden, wieviel an den dunklen und wiedersprechenden Gerüchten Wahres war; genug, Bentonville mußte dafür büßen. Bei unserer Ankunft fanden wir seine Hauptstraßen niedergebrannt und konnten nur aus den rauchenden Trümmern erkennen, daß hier viele bedeuten(de) Kaufläden, Geschäftslokale, Gasthöfe und Kirchen gestanden hatten.

Hierauf kamen zwei andere Städchen an die Reihe.[70] Im ersten derselben hatten die südlichen Truppen ein kleines Hospital zurückgelassen; in dieses drangen einige unserer Cavallerie Offiziere ein und verlangten Branntwein; als entgegnet wurde, es wäre keiner da, musterten sie die Medizinflaschen, glaubten, in einer derselben einen Magenbitter gefunden zu haben, und machten sich darüber her. Offenbar war es eine aus einer einheimischen Giftpflanze bereitete Tinktur; denn in kürzester Zeit traten bey allen, welche davon gekostet hatten, die heftigsten Vergiftungserscheinungen auf; ein Hauptmann verschied; zwey andere Offiziere entgingen mit knapper Noth demselben Schicksal. Unter anderen Verhältnissen hätte man darin eine verdiente Strafe für die Rohheit und Trunkliebe dieser Offiziere erblickt; aber

---

[69] „Küchlein" ist durchgestrichen und „Fladen" darübergeschrieben.
[70] Durchgestrichen: „drei Meilen östlich von unserem Lager gelegen".

im Kriege giebt es kein nüchternes und gerechtes Urtheil, nur Leidenschaft und Aufgeregtheit. Jener Vorfall ist ein schlagendes Beyspiel dafür, wie im Kriege falsche Gerüchte entstehen, wie sie weiter verbreitet und allgemein geglaubt werden, und dazu dienen, Haß und Grausamkeit zu schüren. Im ganzen Norden und selbst in Europa berichteten die Zeitungen, wie in Arkansas Offiziere der Unionsarmee[71] durch vergiftete Lebensmittel umgebracht wurden,

Ende der 44. Manuskriptseite

und nahmen natürlich davon Veranlassung, von der haarsträubenden Barbarei des südlichen Volkes zu sprechen. Dagegen wurde nichts von der Barbarei derjenigen gesagt, deren blinde Wuth jenes Städtchen so wie ein zweites benachbartes in Brand und Asche legte.

Als einige Tage später ein Unteroffizier jener Cavallerie in meiner Gegenwart von dem Vorfall erzählte, frug er, ob wir uns erinnerten, daß sie am Tage unseres Einzugs in Springfield beym Städtchen Little York eine Anzahl Wagen vom feindlichen Train weggenommen und einige der Fuhrleute niedergemetzelt hätten; und als wir dies bejahten, fuhr er fort: „Ich bin ein alter Soldat und nicht gerade weichherzig; aber mir stockte das Blut in den Adern, als uns der kommandierende Offizier befahl, auf die wehrlosen Fuhrleute, alte Männer und Knaben, einzuhauen und er selber den ersten niederschoß. Dieser Offizier war derselbe Hauptmann, welcher an dem Gifte starb. Bei Gott! war das nicht eine Vergeltung?"

Und dies Alles war nur der Anfang des Elends, was über jene Gegend ergehen sollte! Lange, lange noch tobte hier der Orkan des Bürgerkrieges; immer von Neuem stürmten die Schaaren bald der einen, bald der anderen Parthei über diesen Boden, und je länger der Krieg dauerte, desto schonungsloser und erbitterter wurde er geführt. Die beyden Armeen, welche jetzt sich hier gegenüber stunden, waren noch human und wohldisziplinirt zu nennen im Vergleich zu denen, welche nach ihnen kamen und sich in eben dieser Gegend eine Schlacht lieferten. Wahrlich, dies Land mußte zu Ende des Krieges ein Bild der Verwüstung darstellen, ähnlich der Niederungen von Louisiana, wenn die geschwollenen Wasser des Mississippi ihre Dämme durchbrochen und die reichen Plantagen in Sümpfe und Moräste verwandelt haben!

Ende der 45. Manuskriptseite[72]

---

[71] Durchgestrichen: „von Landleuten, deren Gastfreundschaft sie in Anspruch nahmen, vergiftet wurden."

[72] Anmerkung von Klaus Trobisch: Ich finde die Sache hochinteressant und bin froh, dass ich auf diese Weise diesen Text zu lesen kriege. Ich hatte den Amerikanischen

Bürgerkrieg bisher als eine Art Piff-Paff-Spaziergang angesehen und lerne nun dazu. Viele Grüße Klaus.

INDEX

A
adjutant, *vii*
alcohol, *See* beverages
American Indians, 8, 20, 45, 58, 68
animals
   See also game, horse theft
   cattle, 22, 29, 38, 72
   dogs, 23
   horses, *vii*, 13, 21, 26, 28–29, 34, 43, 56, 60, 66, 69, 72
   mules, 8, 11–12, 69
   oxen, 29
   rabbits, 8
architecture, *See* buildings
Army of the Southwest, *ii, iv, vi, xvii*, 5–7, 11, 36
artillery troops, *xi*, 11, 13, 18, 23, 46, 51, 59
Asboth, Alexander, *vi, viii–ix, xi–xiii*, 11, 67
Atlanta, *i*

B
Benton County, 31
Bentonville, *ix, xiii*, 66–67, 70–71, 75
beverages
   See also food
   brandy, 17, 58, 75
   coffee, *xv*, 15–16, 23, 56–59, 72–74
   Jägermeister, 75
   magenbitter, 75
   milk, 58, 73
   tea, 17, 74
   water, 56
   whiskey, 58
   wine, 71
Big Piney River, 18–21
Bolivar, *ix–x*
Brookline, 54
buildings
   See also church, hospital, courthouse
   barracks, *xi, xvii*, 6, 20, 49–52
   farm, 24, 50, 71–72
   frame house, *iv*, 8, 21, 41, 43, 49, 56
   log-house, *xiv*, 8, 14–16, 21, 23, 28, 49–50, 55, 66–67
   shanties, 21
Burns, Ken, *i*
Burns, William S., *viii–xiv*

C
cannon, *xi*, 3, 19–20, 39–40
Carr, Eugene A., *vi*, 12
Cassville, *vi, xii*, 61–62
cavalry, *xi*, 11, 19, 28, 32, 34–35, 39–40, 43, 46, 54, 59, 67, 69, 74–76
Ceatsville, *vi, xii, xiv*, 61
church, 21–22, 61, 75
Corinth, 69
cotton, 7, 71, 73
courthouse, 21, 23–24, 41, 61–62
Cross Hollow, *xiii*
Curtis, Samuel R., *vi, xii*, 7, 34, 36

D
Davis, Jefferson C., *vi*, 12, 36
Der Zerbrochene Krug, 7
Deutscher Kurrentschrift, *iii–v*, 10, 44

disease, *See* illness
divisions, *See specific divisions*
Dixieland, 47
doctor, *vii*, 8, 12, 28, 41, 51
Dulfer, Louis, *xiii*, 75
Dutchmen, *i*

E
Elkhorn Tavern, *xii*, *xv*, 64–65
equestrian, *See* cavalry

F
Ferdinad II, *xv–xvii*
Fifteenth Missouri Volunteer Regiment, *vii–ix*, *xiv*, 5
fire, 38–39, 41, 48, 67
First Division, *ix*, 11, 19, 27, 35–36, 38–40, 47, 52
flag, 28, 41–42
food
    See also beverages, game
    bread, 8, 32, 56–58, 73–74
    corn, 24, 71, 74
    crackers, 16
    eggs, 72–73
    flour, 50, 56, 58, 74
    fruit, 50, 71–72, 74
    lard, 56, 74
    molasses, 8, 73
    pork, 8, 29, 50, 58, 74
    potatoes, 71–72, 74
    wheat, 29, 56, 58, 71, 74
foot soldiers, *See* infantry
forest, *See* landscape
Fort Henry, 37
Fourth Division, 11, 36
Fourth Missouri Cavalry, *viii–xiv*
Fremont, John C., *ii*, *xv–xvii*, 6, 19, 37, 43, 46, 48
Fremont's Bodyguard, *xi*, 46
Fremont Hussars, *viii*

G
Gansevoort, Conrad, *xiii*

game
    See also food
    calf, 56
    fish, 70
    pigs, 15–16, 29, 32, 74
    poultry, 24, 32, 56, 73
    rabbits, 31–32
    sheep, 32, 34, 56
Garibaldi's Southern army, 45–46
Gasconade River, 11, 14, 27
Georgia, 72
Gettysburg, *i*
Grant, Ulysses S., *i*

H
Halleck, Henry W., 6, 46
Hess, Earl, *i*
Hollman, George, *vii*
Hood, John B., 69
hoosiers, *iv*, 19, 31
horse theft, 62–63, 69
hospital, 8, 12, 28, 36, 41, 57, 62, 75
howitzer, 11

I
Illinois, *ii*, 19, 29, 33, 70, 72
illness
    military exemption for, 8–9
    gall fever, 19
    rheumatism, 56
    typhoid, 62
    typhus fever, 19
Indiana, *ii*, 36
Indians, *See* American Indians
infantry, *vii*, *xi*, *xiii*, 5, 11, 19–20, 60, 67, 69, 74
Iowa, *ii*, 22
Italy, 23, 45

J
Jackson, Thomas J. "Stonewall," *i*
Jayhawkers, 69–70

K
Kansas, 45, 55, 69
Keatsville, *See* Ceatsville
Kentucky, 71
Kielmansegge, Eugene von, *viii, xiii*
Kleist, Heinrich von, 7
Kopp, Charles J., *xvii–xviii*, 1–3

L
Lake Erie, 28
landscape
  creek, 14, 18–19, 27, 70
  field, 15, 20, 27, 31–32, 38, 41, 43, 52, 55, 61–62, 67, 70–71
  forest, 18, 20, 32, 38–39, 54, 60–61, 64, 66, 69–71, 74
  gorge, 18–20, 38–39, 64
  hill, 14, 19–20, 36, 38, 41, 49, 52, 61, 64, 66, 70
  mountain, 8, 14, 18, 20–21, 27, 38–39, 64, 69, 71
  swamp, 69, 71, 76
  valley, 18, 20–21, 61–62, 64, 66, 70
Lane, James H., 45
Lebanon, *v*, 27–31, 33–36
Lee, Robert E., *i*
Liberty Tribune, 8, 40
Lincoln, Abraham, *ii, xvi–xvii*
Little Piney River, 14
Little Rock, 71
Little York, *xi*, 54–56, 76
Louisiana, 76
Ludlow, B. C., *viii*
Lyon, Nathaniel, *ii*, 5, 67

M
Marshfield, *v*, 36–37
martial law, *xvi*
McCulloch, Benjamin, 67–69
Mecklenburg, *ix*
Memphis, 22, 69
Mexico, Gulf of, 59

Mississippi River, *i–ii*, 29, 33, 69–70, 76
Missouri River, 5–6, 59
mountain, *See* landscape
music, 1–3, 11, 13–14

N
Native Americans, *See* American Indians
Nebraska, 45
New Orleans, 48
newspaper, *xiii*, 8, 14, 37, 40, 68, 75
North Carolina, 72

O
Ohio, *ii*, 28–29, 45
Osterhaus, Peter J., *vi*, 11
Ozark Mountains, *ix*

P
pack gun, *See* howitzer
Pea Ridge, *i–ii, vi, viii–ix, xii–xiv*, 62, 64–65
Peret, Charles, *vii*
poison, *xiii*, 74–76
Prairie Grove, *i*
Price, Sterling, *ix–xii*, 6–7, 47, 50–51, 53, 59, 67
Pulaski County, 24

Q
quartermaster, *vii*, 12–13, 16–17, 36, 51, 72

R
railroad, 6, 22, 30, 33, 47
Reimers, August, *viii–ix, xiv–xv*
Revolution, German and Hungarian, 45
Richmond, *i*
rivers, *See specific rivers*
Rolla, *v, viii–ix, xiv, xvi–xvii*, 6, 11–13, 18–19, 28–29, 33, 47

138

Rolla Express, 37
Rosecrans, William, 69
Route 66, *v*

S
Schiller, Friedrich, *xv–xvii*, 7, 47
Schwerin, *ix*
Second Division, 6, 11–12, 19–20, 28, 36, 39–40, 47, 52
Second Ohio Battery, *xiii*, 28
Sheridan, Philip H., 13
Sherman, William, *i*, 12
Sigel's division, *See* First Division
Sigel, Franz, *vi*, *xi–xiii*, *xv*, 11, 29, 33–36, 47
slavery, *xvi*, 23, 32, 43, 55, 71–72, 74
Southwest army, *See* Army of the Southwest
Springfield, *v*, *ix*, *xi*, *xv–xvii*, 5–6, 8, 19, 35–36, 40–43, 46–49, 54, 76
Steiger, William, *vii*
St. Louis, *ix*, 5–6, 14, 47, 51, 62
Sugar Creek, *xii–xiv*, 66–67
supplies
　blanket, *xv*, 39, 56, 58
　canister, 58
　coat, *xvii–xviii*, 1–3, 16, 28
　cooking gear, 12, 43, 56, 58
　field bed, 12
　knapsack, *xv*, 12, 39, 46, 50, 52, 56–59
　stove, 12–13, 17
　tent, *ix*, *xi*, *xvii*, 6, 12–13, 15, 17, 20, 27, 34, 46, 52, 55–56, 59–60, 70
surgeon, *See* doctor
Swiss Regiment, 5, 14
Switzerland, 16, 28

T
Tennessee, 69, 72
Texan infantry, 69
Texas, 68, 70

Texas Rangers, 69, 74
theft, 13, 15, 23–24, 29, 32, 43, 48–49, 69, 72, 74–76, *See also* horse theft
Third Division, 11, 36
Third Missouri Volunteer Infantry, *ix*
Thirty Years' War, *xv*
tobacco, 58, 71, 73

U
Utica, 22

V
Vicksburg, *i*
Virginia, 69

W
Wallenstein, *xv–xvii*, 7, 45–47
Washington, 6
Waynesville, *v*, 21–24, 27
weather
　cold, 20, 27, 33, 36, 39, 47, 50, 52–53, 55, 59
　frost, 13, 15, 39, 52, 56–58, 67
　rain, 13, 27, 58–59, 67
　snow, *xiv–xv*, *xvii*, 6, 13–18, 27–28, 47
　warmth, 27–28, 36, 59, 70
West Point, 46
Wilson's Creek, *i–ii*, *ix*, *xii*, *xv*, 5, 41, 52–53, 67
World Wars I and II, *iii*

Z
Zagonyi, Charles, *xi*

www.ingramcontent.com/pod-product-compliance
Lightning Source LLC
Chambersburg PA
CBHW020200090426
42734CB00008B/885